Galveston Wharf Stories

Characters, Captains & Cruises

Alvin L. Sallee

GALVESTON WHARF STORIES

Printed in the United States of America

ISBN: 978-0-9991486-0-0

Revised Edition, 2019

alvinsallee@hotmail.com

Photos:

Cover: Loading dock Galveston wharf,
Imperial Sugar Company
November 7, 1938. Permission: DeGolyer Library,
Southern Methodist University,
Robert Yarnall Richie Photograph Collection.

All other photos by author, unless otherwise noted.

To Nicole and Violet, may you always ask "Why?"
And to the men and women of Galveston
who work the wharves.

Table of Contents

Foreword

It's impossible to know Galveston without knowing something about the port. Islanders say that, but the port remains largely mysterious. Stories are passed down. Jean Laffite, the notorious pirate, sailed to Galveston and is said to have buried treasure before he burned his headquarters and sailed away. During the Civil War, Confederates and Federals fought in the harbor. Later, the most famous Galvestonian of all, Jack Johnson, sharpened his boxing skills as a longshoreman on the docks. He'd become the first African-American to win the heavyweight title. The stories are colorful, but they paint a fragmentary picture of the port.

Alvin Sallee set out to remedy that. He decided it was time to paint a fuller picture.

As you'd expect of a college professor, he did his research. But he also went down to the docks and talked to people. In a series of columns for the *Galveston County Daily News*, he told about people who worked at the port. He talked about sailboats, bulk carriers and cruise ships and boarded a few himself, taking readers on his voyages. He worked with veterans and volunteers who are maintaining the USS *Cavalla* and USS *Stewart,* a submarine and a destroyer escort that fought in World War II. He took jaunts around the harbor with Capt. Vandy Anderson, whose stories about the port and the island were almost limitless. Sadly, Anderson is no longer living. But you can get a sense of the man from reading Alvin's story about a boat ride on a magical day.

As a newspaper editor, I looked forward to reading each weekly installment of Alvin's story. Alvin Sallee is a warm, curious and generous man, and his love for his subject came through with every article.

—Heber Taylor, retired editor *Galveston County Daily News*

For maybe 10 years, I wrote a weekly column for the Galveston paper telling about the Galveston people and their lives of days gone by. That had never been done before, primarily because those stories had long been forgotten by most. It seems to me that when I finally counted them, there were in the neighborhood of 750 of those tales.

A couple of them may have brushed on the Galveston Wharves; one that comes to mind is how Mayor Herbert Y. Cartwright was able to raise the money so the city could buy the wharves from private enterprise. But in the main, I didn't write about the wharves because, even though I was born on the island decades before, I knew very little about them. It's an embarrassing confession.

And I suspect that is a pretty common cultural void among the majority of Galvestonians. I don't know why. I wonder.

Heber Taylor, the editor of the paper, contacted me and asked me if I would mind visiting with Prof. Alvin Sallee the next time he came through Dallas, where I now live. He said Alvin was going to write a series of pieces about the Galveston wharves.

Intriguing, I thought. "Sure, I'd love to meet him."

So, when Alvin arrived at our house for the first time, after several hours, we decided that we were going to be "forever friends," and that we were going to visit every time he came to Dallas.

So, in concert with our handshake agreement, he has sent me each of his columns just before they were published. I love reading them, primarily because he is seeing the wharves' stories as I wish I had.

There are lots of books about Galveston, some pretty good, others not so good.

But whichever of them are among your collection, the whole shooting match will not be complete until you have added Alvin's book about the wharves.

You can trust me on that.

—Bill Cherry author, *Bill Cherry's Galveston Memories*, VanJus Press, 2000

An Interesting Font

This book is set in a font called Cambria. Cambria was the name of a Civil War British ship, a blockade runner, captured by the USS *Huron*. The ship became the federal schooner, USS *Cambria*.

During the battle of Galveston in January, 1863, the *Cambria* was fooled into approaching the Galveston wharves. After the Confederates won the battle Confederate General Magruder had left the U.S. flag up on the new custom house (today found in its original form at Postoffice and 20th Streets). Aboard the *Cambria* were most of the Texans who did not side with the secession. It would have been a Confederate political victory to capture them.

A scouting party sent from the *Cambria* was surprised and seized by the Confederates when they disembarked on Kuhn's Wharf. The party included Thomas "Nicaragua" Smith, a notorious Galvestonian thief and deserter. His request just before the firing squad shot him, was to bury him face down, so the Confederacy could eternally kiss his "behind". (See *Daily News* 3/18/2017, Tom Bassing.) Alerted by the failure of the party's return, the USS *Cambria* was quickly on its way back to U.S. waters.

It was bought later that year in Baltimore for the purpose of sinking. Even a ship named for Wales, USS *Cambria,* visited Galveston. The wharves of Galveston are full of such tales.

Preface: Why This Book?

After a career of addressing one of the worst phenomena in humankind—the physical and sexual abuse of children and worse perhaps, a society which turns its back to them, I chose to write about the positive. I turned to the people and events of the wharves, something I knew a little about, yet was attracted.

While high desert born and raised, I still always felt a connection to salt water. A visiting professorship for four years at the University of Houston–Downtown brought me back to the waters of Galveston, this time to live and begin retirement.

I had read the *Galveston County Daily News*, Texas' oldest newspaper, for years, back to 1975 while on visits. Upon becoming a citizen of Galveston, I subscribed to the paper, reading the community news, editorials and want ads as a treat each evening. I read and then wrote letters to the editor.

Before long I had the opportunity to meet the editor, Mr. Heber Taylor. He asked me to write a column. Given that this allowed me 500 words rather than the 250-word limit for letters, I said yes.

The weekly column evolved into a series on children's issues, presenting the opportunity for me to learn more about the people working with families and children here.

After a year Mr. Taylor suggested a series on the retirement process on which I was about to embark. Another year of columns. Then the announcement one morning over coffee at the Mod Coffee shop that he was retiring. Time for a new series, *Wharf Stories*, which ran for two years each Saturday on the editorial page.

Why Galveston wharf stories?

Fascinated by the Galveston Port, yet ignorant of how it operates, writing a weekly newspaper column would give me a good reason to ask folks for their time and expertise. Learning for free, a novel idea in today's for-profit educational world.

Beginning a new series, one gives thought to a title. The working title was *Wharf Characters*. Hanging out at the docks for the past few years has introduced me to a number of characters, including pelicans down at the Mosquito Fleet. And a rumored reality show (*Big Fish, Texas*) will highlight some wharf characters, and reality shows thrive on personalities.

People and their stories are endlessly interesting, each like a snowflake. The Galveston wharves are a complex system, steeped in the past, politics, engineering and economics—how can you not be interested?

A main character is the wharves themselves. Promoted by none less than Stephen F. Austin as the "best natural harbor in the Texas colony," the Mexican government made Galveston a port of entry. A wharf with a Customs House soon followed and of course, taxes were collected. And through history, right down to today, funding for the wharves continues to be a controversial issue.

Many thanks to too many persons to list who share their stories. To eagle-eye John Moore for proof reading, to Bill Cherry and Heber Taylor for encouraging, to Ted O'Rourke for guiding, to Michael Smith for continuing and to Angela Wilson and all the staff at the *Galveston County Daily News.* And to Capt. Vandy whom we all miss. To the three wonderful women who polished this revised edition: Mari Anderson, Lynne Finley, and especially Kathy Sallee, whose patience proofing and putting up with me is beyond compare.

What you have before you is a collection of columns, most of them first published in the *Galveston County Daily News.* These wharf stories are told by a retired professor, who tried to teach through storytelling.

An old dinghy at the Texas Seaport Museum

We begin in 1971, with the poem about an old wharf-side dinghy I saw as a 21-year-old young man. Now, much older, I have become the dinghy, still watching people who come to the sea. Welcome aboard.

THE DINGHY

Life is a port. Bustled it is love
or a seaside resort.
One pair of lonely eyes
can search in front and beyond
the multitude-filled pier and surmise
ships and boats coming and going
or perhaps bright-eyed bikinied girls
with something showing.
In all this a single dinghy sits, sublime,
riding up and back, to and aft
held to by a long time.
The splintered oars of pulls gone past
now useless but for their rhythmic banging.
A boy's one more cast is made the last
while the tiny crab on granite breakwater lies.
A white sail slows as it enters its slip
while all about the harbor revolve passers-by.
Everything surges gentle like incoming tides
as the last brush stroke of sunlight stretches for
the blue sky before it takes it and hides.
In a useless lighthouse tourists dine, and
later while reading the port-of-call for tomorrow
they buy plastic ships made like pine.
On this eve as those before, in night's soft grays,
paint worn from the seaward side of its life
still on rippled waves the solitary dinghy sways.

—Alvin L. Sallee, 1971

Chapter 1 – Introduction and History

My Version of Galveston Wharf History

Galveston—Somewhere near Texas is a 33-mile slip of sand with a sandy-bottom port. The "best port" on the Gulf of Mexico, uniquely located at the mouth of a Texas sized bay, Galveston Bay, spreading north to Buffalo Bayou and the San Jacinto River. Galveston, the doorway to the Gulf of Mexico and the world.

How did Galveston come to be? The early days.

This is my version of Galveston's wild history. The tall Karankawas were here first. Well, maybe after the snakes. Then came the Spanish calling the place appropriately Snake Island (Isla de Culebras). Frenchman La Salle in 1685 renamed it the San Louis. Over the next few hundred years the spot morphed from Campeche into the name Galvez-towm (yes, m) to Galveston.

Pirates

Speaking of names, after aiding General Andrew Jackson at the Battle of New Orleans, which ended the war of 1812, the Lafitte (that is how they spelled it) brothers—Antoine, Jean and Pierre—were no longer welcome in the Crescent City's high society. Leaving New Orleans in 1817 they sailed west to the next best port, Galveston. Louis-Michel D'Aury, another French slave trading pirate, preceded the Lafittes, but soon departed for parts east—Spanish Florida.

Campeche became Lafitte's town and grew to a fairly organized group of a thousand rum and slave smugglers. Jim

Bowie, of Alamo fame, bought slaves from Lafitte in Galveston and turned them in for a reward at the border of Louisiana, U.S.A., once making $65,000. The suave Jean Lafitte's two-story home, La Maison Rouge, stood at what is now Harborside Drive between 14th and 15th Streets. Even today the bottom stone story of a home built on his house's footing still stands. A replica of his ship, the *Pride*, can be found in the aquarium at Moody Gardens.

In 1821, the U.S. Navy showed up and invited the pirates to exit and destroy everything. They did, after burning the town and wharf to the ground and water respectively. No one knows where they went or if they really buried their treasure at the base of three trees. The legend remains. (Check Stewart Road at 91st Street.)

A Republic is born

Just two years later American colonists under Moses and his son Stephen F. Austin were on the scene. Galveston was then part of a new country, Mexico.

Before long GTT (Gone To Texas) signs were left throughout the southern states, as colonists left the U.S.A. for Galveston and points west.

Santa Anna, the ruler of Mexico, established a Customs House on the east end of Galveston. The long wooden wharves appeared stretching out from the shallow shore to deeper water. Galveston began to grow.

"Remember the Alamo" echoed in Galveston in 1836 as Texans fought for independence and to maintain slavery. Santa Anna charged east across the Texas countryside as Texas President Burnett fled to Galveston, to the Customs House, and waited for the worst.

Unknown to the Texas government at the time, General Houston had trapped Santa Anna on the north shore of Galveston Bay. Santa Anna was preoccupied with the "Yellow Rose of Texas" in his tent, or so the story goes. The Texans won the day. Wounded, Gen. Sam and the captured Santa Anna came through Galveston on their way back from the battle.

The Republic stood.

The first Daughters of the Republic of Texas (DRT)chapter was named for Sidney Sherman. His statue stands on Broadway and 7th Street. The chapter house, known as the Cradle, is at 29th Street and Avenue O½. It was the library of William Pitt Ballinger's home. His daughter, Miss Betty, was a co-founder of the organization in 1891. The DRT is still going strong, in fact my sister-in-law is going to join in her retirement.

Doorway to the Largest State

Only a few years later the Lone Star Republic, Texas, joined the United States in 1845 as the 28th state. A slave state, the largest in the Union. Galveston was the largest city and had slaves working in dining rooms, the fields and on the wharves.

Galveston's port and city took off—cotton and immigration created churches, banks and a thriving customs business. Peoples from all over the world traveled by sea to the blooming port city. A multicultural wave, including slaves, came across the many wharves to the city.

One of the wharves can be found at 20th Street., today known as J.C. Kuhn's wharf, built in 1838 by Colonel Ephrain McLean. Ship owners Handley and Kuhn welcomed steam ships from around the world across their wharf. Regular visits came from Liverpool, England.

Bondage and Liberation: Civil War

In April, 1861 Sam Houston, the just-resigned governor of Texas, crossed the Galveston wharves again, this time to warn of the dangers and cost of secession. He faced a hostile crowd. His dire predictions for his beloved State became true as Texans not killed in the Civil War came home at the point of Union bayonets.

Kuhn had sold his share of the wharf and headed for England in 1861. Yet his wharf played a critical role in the Battle of Galveston. The U.S. Navy tied up ships at the end of the wharf. During the day, Union forces marched through the city, often to the new U.S. Custom House at 21st and Postoffice streets. They returned to safety in the warehouse at the end of the wharf each evening.

Confederate Maj. Gen. McGregor, on the night of January 1, 1863, led his forces up to the foot of Kuhn's wharf to attack the Union forces on the wharf. The Union troops each night removed a section of boards on the wharf leaving only one board lengthwise in place to cross over.

The Confederate forces brought ladders to climb onto the wharf from the water but found the ladders were too short. The Southern soldiers retreated back behind the Hendley Building at 20th Street and The Strand. Confederate "cotton-clads" came to the rescue from the bay. After a U.S. Navy ship was sunk, the Union forces withdrew from Galveston for the rest of the war. Until the recent remodeling of the Hendley Building in 2016, scars from the shells fired by the Union Navy could still be seen on one of the granite lintels.

After the end of the war, on June 19, 1865, the abolition of slavery was proclaimed in Galveston. Juneteenth is still celebrated each year, not only in Galveston but throughout Texas and across the country. As James M. Schmidt wrote, Galveston provided the bookends of slavery, "the cruelties of bondage and the promise of liberation."

Reconstruction and Jim Crow

The wharves helped Galveston recover faster than most other communities in the Confederacy. While not all Galveston wharves have such deep roots in history, they do have stories to tell.

The plight of black people improved in Galveston as well—what else could happen after slavery? Largely through the efforts of two gentlemen, George Ruby and Norris Wright Cuney, former slaves made progress. Mr. Cuney, the son of a white colonel and a slave mistress, played a major role in race and wharf relationships from the Civil War until his death at age 51 in 1898.

Mr. Cuney allied with a former Confederate colonel, William Moody, who was president of the Cotton Exchange, to break the strike of white longshoremen in 1885 by bringing in black "scab" workers. The union wages dropped from 50 to 40 cents an hour. Police protection was deemed necessary for Cuney and his laborers. But blacks now had a union. Today the two unions are one.

With the end of Reconstruction came Jim Crow policies, almost a caste system for former slaves. There were separate schools until 1968, long after Brown vs. Topeka Board of Education and the Civil Rights Act.

Public housing was torn down almost immediately after Hurricane *Ike* in 2008, relocating part of the black community off the Island. Low income housing has still not fully returned almost 10 years later.

At the height of the Jim Crow era, a dockworker, Galveston Giant Jack Johnson, reigned as the heavyweight boxing champion of the world. As Ken Burns stated, Jack Johnson was the most famous African-American on earth for 13 years. Later, falsely accused of violating the Mann Act, he still retained his esteemed place in Galveston.

Today, Nathan, a black man, refers to me as Mr. Alvin. As we became closer friends I asked him why. He replied, "My mother told me to always refer to people in that manner." My guess is "people" were white people. I am not comfortable with this salutation but respect his wishes.

In my observation, most African-Americans in Galveston don't stand on equal economic ground with whites, even after all this time. In my columns, I referred to black supervisors or leaders by race. The editors said that race should be used only if it is necessary to the story. Given the southern roots which remain in Galveston, I think it's probably always necessary.

The first public swimming pool finally came to Galveston 2017, over a century after the Civil War was fought over slavery and Jim Crow segregation of even the beach.

Galveston: An Economic Engine Meets the Great Storm

After the Civil War, immigrants poured over the wharves into the city. Their places on the ships taken by cotton as it was quickly stowed into every nook on the vessels before they sailed. Immigrants were charged low fares so the ships could be packed with cotton as the ships returned to Europe.

Elissa, now the official tall ship of Texas, called here twice. In 1884 she brought bananas and left with cotton for England. Today she sails out of Pier 22 as the oldest active barque in the U.S.

During the 1870s and 1880s, sand bars continued to hinder ships entering the wharves. Galveston slipped to literally a third-class port with a depth of less than 20 feet. A deep-water harbor with jetties was needed.

Every political chip was called due, and after all the federal and state wheeling and dealing, Galveston became a world class port by 1898. It was second only to Liverpool, England, in cotton shipments. One historian wrote, "It is doubtful if any port in the world attained such prominence in such a short time."

By 1900, 1,200 ships called upon Galveston each year. The city boasted 20 hotels, 60 factories and 37,000 residents. The Strand, the name transported as well from England, was booming, known as the Wall Street of the South. More millionaires lived here per capita than in any other city in the U.S.A. The new medical school, the University of Texas Medical Branch (UTMB), opened in "Old Red," designed by famous Galvestonian architect Nicolas Clayton in 1891. Also by 1900, Galveston had electricity throughout the community, flush toilets in many homes, street cars powered by electricity and giant steam engines pulling railcars all along the wharves. Galveston wharves accounted for 70 percent of United States cotton exports.

Tallship of Texas, Elissa, off Galveston

Despite fires and epidemics since the 1860s, by Sept. 7, 1900, Galveston could be envied by almost any city in the United States. Galveston was it, going strong, the 1894 Grand Opera House and all.

The Great Storm

The next day, Sept. 8, 1900, up to 8,000 citizens were dead with thousands more injured, 10,000 homeless and more than 3,000 homes destroyed. The Great Storm had struck. The worst natural disaster in the history of the United States hammered Galveston in the form of a hurricane.

As Al Roker wrote regarding passengers arriving in the port the next day, "They saw the docks collapsed, boats wrecked, the greatest shipping port in Texas, one of the grandest in the nation, even in the world, now had no wharf."

The world responded with aid. Clara Barton of the Red

Cross arrived with lumber, and the rebuilding of Galveston began. The wharves were quickly rebuilt, helping the economy to recover quickly.

The silver lining in the storm was that the heavy rain stretched over Texas created the best soil conditions in years. Cotton was planted on every possible acre, which created a bumper crop in 1901. Every bale was hauled over Galveston's wharves by former slaves in huge wheelbarrows. Galveston was back in the money, for a year.

As Galveston author Bill Cherry tells it, the storm also brought boll weevils from the Yucatán. They ate through the cotton the next year and the credit of many farmers evaporated as the leaves fell off their cash crop.

Rebuilding

Rabbi Henry Cohen began the "Galveston Movement" in 1907 and over the next seven years 10,000 Eastern European Jewish immigrants came through Galveston. Most met with the rabbi personally for guidance and then moved to central Texas and beyond. Rabbi Cohen served Galveston from 1886-1949. He influenced many public policies, among them raising the age of sexual consent for girls from 10 years old to 18.

Despite the efforts of the rabbi and others, as the city recovered it became even more "open". As a worldly, unrestricted seaport, Galveston entertained a bit more of a tolerant environment. Gambling, bawdy houses on Postoffice Street, speakeasies, all manner of social ills.

Depression, Free State and Historic Preservation

Galveston weathered the Great Depression of the 1930s a bit easier than the rest of the country, largely due to its wharves and conservative bankers. Galvestonians began to diversify—air conditioning to the rescue. The beach, new exotic hotels and clubs with the wharves helped bring millions of tourists to the island. The "free state" of Galveston reigned with all vices until 1957.

Once again, Galveston adjusted, this time by offering family-friendly attractions. Today the Seaport Museum, Seawolf Park, dozens of private attractions and cruise ships bring more than six million visitors per year to the wharves and beaches.

Bill Cherry adds that a barrier island just is not designed by nature to put industrial centers on. What works on the mainland is not applicable to the strip of sand off the coast.

Hurricanes continued to hit the island from 1915 until present. On Sept. 12, 1961, Hurricane Carla visited Galveston. This time it was documented on television by a young reporter, Dan Rather, and local radio newsman Vandy Anderson. While Carla barely missed Galveston, tornadoes traveled from the Pleasure Pier north along 23rd Street to the wharves. Even today, evidence of Carla's destruction can be seen in the less than attractive 1960's architecture.

George Mitchell, an A&M graduate, oilman and developer of The Woodlands, went on in the 1970s to save The Strand by renovating many historical buildings. The causeway, which brings millions to the island, is rightfully named for Cynthia and George Mitchell.

The 1960s began the "tear it down" era in Galveston. Fortunately, urban renewal was halted in the 1970's by the Galveston Historic Foundation and Galveston citizens.

The Wharves Board in 1977 proposed to eliminate the "Mosquito Fleet", shrimp and charter boats from Piers 19 and 20. The Board wanted to convert this historic area to cargo ship wharves. The Board's referendum nonetheless was defeated by the citizens. The "Mosquito Fleet" can still be found at what was the end of Kuhn's wharf today. Even now, sloops and schooners are tied to the wooden wharves. I know, I walked the dogs this morning across the boards in a light fog.

Citizen efforts were required again after Hurricane *Ike* struck on September 13, 2008, arriving through the back door from the bay, flooding the Strand under 10 feet of water. Several pieces of "*Iked*" furniture now furnish our home.

Sometimes we suffer from hurricane amnesia in Galveston. A critically needed *Ike Dike* is still in the beginning planning stages almost 10 years later. After the 1900 Great Storm, without computers and huge equipment, the seawall was constructed in just four years.

Higher Education on the Island

One job creator that does work on an island is higher education, beginning with the University of Texas Medical Branch in 1891, the first medical school west of the Mississippi. Texas A&M University, Galveston, including a maritime academy, opened in 1962. Now on Pelican Island, on land donated by George Mitchell, it continues to grow. Galveston Community College, rated the best in Texas, began on Avenue Q in 1967.

What makes Galveston Resilient?

Over the years, Galveston's people have recovered even faster than its economy. Resiliency may have been invented here. Storm after storm, challenge after challenge, the community responds. The few very wealthy families of Galveston have given back to meet the needs of others over and over again. Leadership has been provided creating new forms of government, like the deep-water committee that led to today's wharves. Families have put collective needs first, if not always to perfection.

It is people who make Galveston. It is the women, from community leaders to the famous red light district, women have shaped Galveston. Mrs. Ruth Kemper, the wife of a major business owner, was the first woman elected to the city council in 1960, mostly with support from the madams of the houses of prostitution on Postoffice Street. Only in Galveston.

There are other barrier islands all along the Texas Coast, yet there is only one Galveston. Whether a BOI (Born on the Island) or IBC (Islander by Choice) a doctor or dockworker, black or white, Muslim, Christian or Jew, or just characters, people pull together for Galveston in a crisis. Other times, maybe not so much. Then it is who you know.

Through it all, shaped by the land or attracted by the water, there have always been big and interesting personalities on Galveston Island. No group of 50,000 people equals the energy, chutzpah and resolve.

For me, it all began at the waterfront, the wharves. Even today millions of people are drawn here. Personalities, whether by tolerance or choice, are found along the wharf. As long as the seas continue to be the largest, most used method of transportation, then hope will cross the wharf every day going and coming through Galveston.

Chapter 2 - Wharf Setting

Often Mentioned Fog

As I read over the hundred plus columns which comprise this book, I found a number of them reference fog. Looking out the window just now, I see fog whisking in. Fog stalks the coastline clogging ports every winter for days at a time. Fog can close the Houston port the equivalent of half to a full month each year. That costs time, and since time is money it is expensive.

The theme of fog along wharves is found in the lives of pilots, port operations, cruise ship headquarters, hotels, 18-wheelers and buses. During fog attacks, Port Coordination Team (PCT) meetings are held each morning at 9 a.m. with all interested parties. The PCT includes the U.S. Coast Guard, tug boat, oil, shipping, and fueling companies plus ship's agents and security agencies.

One critical factor most of us landlubbers don't know about is the MARAD, the Maritime Administration. This government agency is charged with keeping a strong merchant marine including being able to support our military deployments. Not something we want to do in a fog.

The members of the PCT prioritize which vessels will come and go when the fog lifts. Cruise ships and produce vessels are usually at the top of the list. Until then, ships remain tied to the wharf or find anchorage off-shore. During the meetings pilots have a great deal of influence. They have the experience to know what sight limits are necessary along the channels which vessels must take from the sea buoy to the wharves.

There are numerous examples of ship captains trying to make a fast turn-around and pilots disagreeing. One Galveston pilot had to hold his ground by stopping a ship inbound one morning until the fog lifted. When the fog slipped away two kayakers were spotted just clearing the channel. A close call for them and they probably didn't even know about it.

One recent Saturday, Mo, a friend from Houston, called late in the afternoon and asked if she could stay in our spare apartment that night. She explained that the fog had come in so thick she could not drive back to Houston. There were no rooms available in town. Two cruise ships were stuck off-shore and all the folks who were leaving that day had no place to stay. What a mess, and this is just one day and two ships.

Fog helped to close the beautiful new Houston Cruise ship terminal in Baytown for good. After only two years the two cruise lines using it cancelled their contracts due to fog-related costs. Steaming two hours up a narrow channel across the Bay cost enough, but adding additional fog-related expenses was too much. Unlike the Port of Galveston there are no hotels or restaurants by the Houston Port, just container wharves. The fog won.

Fog brings a mysterious feel to events, such as the story about the Old San Juan, Puerto Rico, guard who disappeared in the night fog. Or war ships, from Civil War sailing schooners to German U-boats during the Second World War, moving into the fog off the coast.

What is this stuff called fog? It's a thick cloud of tiny water droplets suspended in the atmosphere near the earth's surface, according to one source. Sort of takes the romance out of the feeling one gets standing on board a ship, gray everywhere, fog horn sounding in the distance.

Of course, there is always the concept of one's mind being in a fog. This state came over me a number of times while settling into the routine aboard a cruise ship. Is this a sea day or will we dock, and if so where? I wonder.

So, all of this is to ask for your understanding for any overuse of setting the scene for many columns in the fog. Along the coast fog is often present, whether in the air or in my mind.

The fog is lifting now as I finish this piece. Ship's agents, owners and dock workers are relieved. Life on the wharf can resume on schedule.

Fog keeps cruise ship at wharf

The Hub of the Port—Ship's Agent

What almost two hours? The poor man hardly had time to eat his sandwich. His answers cascade with the intricacies of his job. Time to cast off another ship, so we head out of Rudy and Paco's restaurant, saying "Hi" to Lyle Lovett on our way.

Even in the space age, the oceans are the highways of the world, transporting everything from autos to sulfur to ports from Lagos to San Diego.

Once in the harbor, the ship's agent represents the ship owner. Agents are the hub of the ship's port call. Arrangements include, a pilot, tugboats, line handlers—union or non—stevedores, equipment on the ship and wharf, customs, immigration, social services, fuel barge, security, employment services, shore transportation and occasionally a shopping trip for the ship master's wife. Did I mention statutory authorities for inspections and certifications on the ship? Beginning his job as a ship's agent 17 years ago, across from wharf 24, George Christie comments he now has the routine down to the point where a monkey could do it. According to one survey, there are up to 130 separate operations an agent may have to undertake for one ship's visit. It takes about five years to learn. Must be a smart monkey.

From bureaucratic forms to chitchat, the details of coordination begin before the ship arrives and continues non-stop, thanks to email and cell phones, until the agent shakes hands with the Master and walks off the gangplank.

Remember, each of these interactions take place with people, not unemotional computers. People have personalities. There are good days and not so good days, favorites and not-so-much. Mix in millions of dollars in transactions, insurance, different rules depending on the ship's flag, and the need for close teamwork by competing businesses. Ships only make money when they are moving, so time matters. Did I mention stress?

A day in the life. A tugboat needs to position a ship next to the wharf. The current is strong so it takes longer than planned. The line handler's company has to pay their workers to stand around waiting, thus not making money. Would you like to referee that debate? Me neither.

Or the Coast Guard calls you and says they arrested a ship from Cuba with tons of cocaine, can you find a wharf fast? You do and as you go up the gangway, you have an M16 pointed at your chest by an ATF agent. You calmly push the barrel down and explain that as the ship's agent you need to board. When the barrel is raised again, you leave and make several phone calls.

Pirates are boarding ships sailing from Galveston off Lagos, robbing sailors and taking food. The ship company comes up with a plan. As the agent, you must "gift wrap" a large "grocery bag" of wonderful Texas food, including 800 pounds of beef so the pirates take the "grocery bag" and nothing else. The plan works. Here comes the next ship around Fort Point.

Southside of Port of Galveston from Pier 21

Airplanes, Airstreams and Boats on the Wharf

Each morning, driving over the Harborside viaduct (definition, overpass), I look down to see if the Hoegh ship is in this week. This enormous straight-sided ship is a large box with a flat top deck and a small bridge aft. Known as a RO/RO (roll-on, roll-off) ship, I haven't seen it for a while.

Later touring with Ted O'Rourke, I explore Pier 34, home of one of the RO/RO wharves. RO/RO is an important business on the wharf. The concept began in 1849 by rolling railcars on a barge. Come to find out my dad commanded a RO/RO, a Landing Ship Tank (LST), in the Philippines after World War II. LSTs, slightly longer than USS *Stewart*, drew only three feet even with several tanks aboard. Beached, the bow opened up, a ramp dropped down and off rolled tanks and other wheeled vehicles. Continuing to drive around, we see acres of vacant land, yet RO/RO effect is still evident. We meet Bob Martin as he applies bar codes on cars waiting to roll on. He also builds surfboards. Half-mile wide concrete and gravel parking lots sit next to the wharves from 10th Street to 39th. Finger piers have been filled in, creating more space for anything on wheels you can imagine.

Ports American's Jay Cromie should know. As he puts it, when something goes wrong, he is the last person standing. Sounds like the number one guy to me. Hoegh, he clarifies, left last month for Freeport.

One windmill blade sits off to the side. A few weeks ago, the area was covered with blades and towers being offloaded by moving cranes. Placed on specially fitted railroad cars, they were off to West Texas. For years, even before *Ike*, a smart looking two-door BMV car sat on the wharf. The last few years it was against the fence right across from UTMB. Rolled off a ship from Germany,the BMW failed the emissions test required by California, its intended future home. Lacking funds to meet standards, the owner left it "out of the country", on the wharf, BMW no man's land. When the new BMW plant on Pier 10 came to life, it was moved. Wonder where? Anyone for an "*Ike'd*" 2007 Beemer? The BMW could be a symbol of the port. Long lasting, yet always changing to meet new forms of the least expensive mode of transporting large items. Able to RO/RO anything put on wheels, even airplanes, Airstreams and boats.

Seagull II with Captain Brian leaves Fisherman's Wharf

Port Introduction by Capt. Vandy Anderson

"Hey, would you hand me that book?" What was he thinking? The logbook was within his reach. He was a commanding fellow, with a voice to match. So, I hand him the book over the short couple of feet that separates us. This was my first Galveston harbor cruise on *Seagull II* in many years and my first with a BOI (Born on the Island) legend, Captain Vandy Anderson.

This little incident spoke volumes about this multifaceted gentleman. With a nonchalant form from years of experience, he steered the 48-foot boat, easily clearing the pier. In a made-for-radio-hall-of-fame voice, he began an informative lecture on the ship *Elissa*, the port, and the oil blowout valve. He mentioned Galveston is the only town with both the University of Texas and Texas A&M campuses. (Maybe they could play a football game here sometime?)

As we headed out for the channel to look for dolphins, he took a break from his commentary. This provided me the opportunity to mention to him that I really appreciated the manner in which he served as Master of Ceremony at several charity events we had attended on the island.

He shared he was retired and did the harbor cruises a few times a week. Carefully and as tactfully as possible I inquired as to the credentials necessary to be a Captain of the Seagull II. He said it was pretty easy—you needed to pass a test and have over a year of sea days.

On the way back to the wharf, Capt. Vandy explained why he had asked me to hand him the book. "There, that is an hour of sea duty for you. As captain, I asked you to do something and you did it," he said.

Given that I was working 60-hour weeks, time for sea days was limited. So I asked if riding the Galveston ferry would count too, if I got in my car when the ferry captain asked me to. Capt. Vandy's answer: "No." I did not venture to ask him about days on cruise ships watching the bridge on closed circuit TV.

While what seemed easy, steering the tour boat, was really multifaceted. Clearly, I did not have a clue of what was required to captain a tour. The first of many Capt. Vandy concise lessons which I learned.

Wharf Story Source

There would be no Wharf Story series without Captain Vandy Anderson ... and now he is gone. We just had our usual lunch at his table in Rudy and Paco's Thursday before last. Whenever mystified by the wharves or someone, I lunched with Capt. Vandy. Frequently, he picked up the tab and always had an answer.

We met years ago. He was the captain of the Seagull II, I was a wide-eyed tourist. In 2010, we had an in-depth conversation while puttering around the harbor, as he explained the complexity of the port and shipping operations.

When I asked what it took to become a captain, he handed me the logbook and asked me to hand it back to him. Puzzled, I complied. "Now," he said. "After about a year at sea, you can sit for the test to become a captain." This was classic Vandy, straightforward with a lesson that stuck.

The past four years, we met for lunch—Rudy and Paco's, same table, same day (Thursday), same time, once or twice a month. At times, someone else would join us, and each of us guests left feeling we had been the center of Vandy's attention.

Vandy was the "talking encyclopedia" of Galveston, both past and present. As the leaders in our town walked in to the restaurant, he would gently wave them over to the table and introduce me. After a brief visit, they would join their own tables, then Vandy would share their histories and contexts with me. Just as he did on his broadcasts, his stories were punctuated by smiling acknowledgement. Countless column ideas were generated during each lunch.

Every so often a positive email note about a particular column would arrive. He treated me and everyone with respect, patiently answering even uninformed questions.

In one column draft I wrote, "The main thing the Pelican Bridge holds up is progress." Remembering that Capt. Vandy chaired the Navigation Commission, which oversees the bridge, I thought maybe he should read the draft. He shot back an email asking why I would say that about the bridge? He was correct—it is not the bridge holding up progress on Pelican Island.

During our last lunch, he was pleased with progress toward building a new bridge. When it is built, I move it be named the "Capt. Vandy Anderson Memorial Bridge." Maybe then we can all pick up the tab.

Going Cosmopolitan at the Wharf

Cruising down Broadway, sipping my Cambodian Happy Coffee on my ritual Saturday morning trip to Chalmers Hardware, I look down 31st street and see the *Triumph* cruise ship parked bow in.

Well that changes my day, appetizers this afternoon at 4:00 on Fisherman's Wharf, not sailing with Captain Kidd in Kemah. Will reschedule that trip. Watching the *Triumph* rotate in the Galveston Port is never to be missed.

Once on a tour of the *Carnival Triumph's* bridge, I commented that the ship must have a very exact GPS to turn in such a tight spot. The captain in an "I am insulted voice" exclaimed that "he, not the computer steered the ship"—oops.

This morning while standing on the Galveston wharf staring up at the newly arrived fourteen-story skyscraper, I try to figure out where our cabin will be on our next trip. Walking off the ship, a tall young African-American man looks up from his cell phone. I ask if he knows where the forward ADA cabin is located. He explains the layout and we count up to 12 decks and I see it, I think.

Knowing he wants to get ashore, I find out he is "Chicago Chris", one of only nine trumpet players in the Carnival ship family. Once he wore jeans to a jam session in Chicago and got chewed out. Chicago is old style jazz; formal suits only.

Good to know, I think, if I'm playing jazz in Chicago, since this morning I'm wearing my old shorts and red Bark in the Park, Adopt-Don't-Shop t-shirt. Chris, in shorts too, hurries off as I say, "See you on board." He's not in Chicago anymore.

That afternoon digging into my crab queso, I see linemen casting off each rope. Jumping up to snap some pictures, I hear a couple of gentlemen next to me speaking Chinese (I think). One asks me in perfect English, "Why don't they just back out?"

I explain that the *Triumph* is only 893 feet long, so they turn around here at the port.

Then I begin to wonder. This will be tight. There are a lot of jack-up rigs across the way constricting the harbor even more.

I add, "The longer ships, over a thousand feet, must back down to the yacht basin before rotating." Telling him about my brief visit with the *Triumph* captain, I conclude, "It is amazing." Continuing to speak in English, he agrees and then returns to his conversation in Chinese. A couple sits down next to me. I hear a heavy British accent.

Trying not to eavesdrop, impossible sitting shoulder to shoulder, I overhear their excited tête-à-tête. They just arrived this morning on the ship and are spending the day in Galveston. While they are busy reviewing their plans, I ask for the check.

While staring at the sea doesn't get you anywhere, hanging out at Pier 21 does allow the world to come to you. Everyday, folks from all corners of the earth come through Galveston. Some even stay. Diversity is another wonderful benefit of the Galveston wharves to our small island.

Going Bananas on the Wharf

Well, not just bananas, also watermelons, pineapples, honeydew, and my favorite, plantains. The sizeable Del Monte ships arrive weekly at the wharf from Central America filled with tropical fruits. The produce passes through Galveston County and all points north, all the way to Canada.

For years, standing outside the fence or on the Seagull II, I wondered what went on in those buildings. Thanks to Ted O'Rourke and many other members of the ILA—International Longshoremen's union—now I know.

Ted pulls up to the Pier 18 gate greeted by a friendly port police officer. I proudly hand the officer my new TWIC card in its plastic cover. My first time being "TWIC'd". The officer puts the plastic card in a slot on his hand-held-device and after a few tense (for me) seconds he smiles and hands it back. Ted kids him about his new mustache. Looks good to me.

We circle by a maintenance garage where truck trailers are

repaired. Pulling up to a silver colored building, we head in, where we are again warmly welcomed. This space is home to more than 60 small electric forklifts and a few golf carts.

In an interior office, computers whirl, printouts shoot out data—farm source, types and details. Rene Ewald is the only woman in sight. Having worked here five years she really likes it, explaining she feels respected. Cursing is not allowed in her office.

Ted asks to borrow a golf cart. Good move, this wharf is vast and my legs don't work as well as when I ran marathons. Unplugged, we're off to the Del Monte banana building, the one we can see from the UTMB parking structure.

We walk into a lengthy covered breezeway connecting the back of open semi-truck trailers with huge refrigerators. From here that is all you can see. No trucks, just the opening as if in a long hallway. Years ago, this area was open. Bananas had to be pushed up ramps into the trucks by hand. Now the electric powered forklifts rush back and carrying pallets fashioned to fit perfectly into the trailers. As the forklifts approach the giant garage doors, they magically open. We quickly follow. The racks in this refrig go several stories high. The forklift grabs a pallet and rushes back under the opening door into the trailer.

Mr. Lloyd George, a dignified African-American gentleman with graying hair, stands at the rear of the trailer with another hand-held device, scanning each pallet's bar code. Little did I know when I was a college student working at Baldridge Hardware in 1969, that the IBM barcodes I pasted on shelves would evolve to run the world of bananas. And everything else. Mr. George has seen major changes too, during his 30 years on the wharf.

From this sanitary enclosed space, we head out to the "parking lot". More than 600 trucks pass through here each week backing up to one of the 32 custom-designed doorways to receive 1,160 boxes of fruit. Then they are off. Now I'm hungry for plantains. Hello, Happy Coffee Shop.

Sentinels of the Ports—Harbor Pilots

It is 1838. Two sloops race out of Galveston Bay toward a ship arriving from New Orleans. Who can get there first? Shots ring out as this contest is about money. The first pilot to board the ship will receive payment, the others, nothing but time at sea. Or so legend has it.

Known as the best port on the Texas coast, Galveston became the Wall Street of the South, largely through shipping. Cotton was shipped out and goods of all types came in through the ever-changing channel. Currents shifted sand bars in Bolivar Roads and the Sabine-Freeport current was difficult to judge. Even with today's technology, the trip is dangerous and requires extensive experience.

A better process to pilot ships to Galveston was so critical that the second state agency created by Texas regulated pilots. Since 1845, Galveston pilots have served as Sentinels of the Port. The pilot provides critical information to the ship's master (the captain) from the sea buoy to the pier. The captain is in control of the ship, except in the Panama Canal.

According to state law the mission of the Galveston-Texas City Pilots is "to guide vessels safely to their berths or out to sea. A pilot's primary responsibility is to protect the public interest of the State of Texas by facilitating the safe and efficient movement of vessels in state waters by exercising independent judgment to protect the property, lives, environment and the economic well-being of the ports of Galveston County."

This paragraph addresses many possible conflicts of interest. Ship owners need to dock and unload as soon as possible, then get another cargo. Who determines when each ship can enter the port? Who makes the rules to regulate trade so the public is served? Who creates the rules and enforces them?

These questions faced the first Texas Legislature. The solution is found in the Transportation Code, Title 4: Navigation. In a few pages of legalese are all the directions for establishing and operating the Board of Pilot Commissioners. Appointed by the Governor and confirmed by the Senate. The present Board is Eddie Janek, Brad Boney, Henry Porretto,

Linda Rounds, and Chair Vandy Anderson.

The Board sets the rules and oversees the pilots, who umpire disputes. Like umpires, we often do not notice them, unless something goes wrong. Normal transportation operations consist of a number of tensions, which may cause accidents. Safety vs. Profit. Time vs. Risk. Ships vs. Nature—wind and currents. Speed vs. Conditions. U.S. Regulations vs. Flags of Convenience. After input, the Board and Pilots develop rules to address these conflicts.

Our umpires, the Galveston-Texas City Pilots, guide over 5,000 ship maneuvers safely every year. And when something goes wrong, they quickly figure out how to fix it to protect our environment, economy and us.

Tolerance, Understanding Cross the Wharf Every Day

"You are taller than I thought," is the surprise reaction I often receive from readers the first time we meet in person. The comment is so unusual that I began exploring why the misunderstanding.

Do I write short? Normally the editor runs my column long down the right side of the page, top to bottom. No, that's not it.

Do I look short in my picture? The camera was clearly below me. Do comments about Pilates making me taller lead one to think I was short to begin with? What about banging my head on historical ships?

At six feet three—not that tall—with a 36-inch inseam, there are days I wish I were smaller. Wedging into a plane seat, finding long pants (another plus for Galveston's weather where one can wear shorts) and fitting into a car are all challenges.

While incorrect assumptions regarding my height are rather minor, it got me thinking. What about more significant misconceptions?

When we have a belief not based on experience or knowledge often it results in harm and incorrect judgment.

It's called prejudice.

Our country, indeed the world, seems very divided and

fueled by unknowns. The list is long: gay marriage, women in power, no college ID's for voting, immigrant children born in the US, choice, guns, bathrooms, unemployment, socialism, among dozens of issues found in the paper every day. Facts and reason don't matter, fear motivates.

When did we Americans become such scaredy-cats? The Depression did not petrify us with fear. "The only thing we have to fear is fear itself," FDR said. Then the greatest generation led us to victory in World War II.

After that maybe we should have dreaded conflicts more before we entered. Yet, the men and women who actually sacrificed did not panic.

Civil Rights leaders did not let terror take them, while bullets did. In the Charleston mass murder, church members did not let fear turn into hate.

Seems like the majority of those who are insecure look like me: older white men, perhaps shorter. With out of proportion alarmism, politicians on all sides fan worries of equality, shared governance and honest wealth.

Of the folks I know on the wharf, those least afraid are those who have traveled the most. They have seen it all and know how considerably better we have it than others. Whether they served in the military or not, they bravely face the wharf each day.

For over 150 years those who passed through the Port of Galveston controlled uncertainties with optimism. Some were met by Rabbi Cohen, others traveled inland alone. Those who came before built a new Republic under Sam Houston, another fearless and broadminded individual.

When intolerance and fear rule, we ignore evidence and vote against our self-interests and values.

Perhaps the most valuable commodity which comes across the wharf is tolerance and understanding. This Fourth of July, maybe we should increase these cargoes.

Bill Cherry: The Grand Old Author of Galveston

Detail every red brick in the wall at the beginning of a column. When initiating a story let the reader know exactly what you were seeing. Of course, have a beginning, middle and end, with a moral to the story. Then you will have a good column. Now I had my answer to what makes a newspaper column worth reading.

I was sitting in Bill Cherry's world headquarters, also known as his den. In fact, he does live in a red brick house, which seems to meander for several miles back to this very comfortable setting. Surrounded by large live oaks on a beautiful green lawn in North Dallas it seems far from the beaches and history of Galveston for this, the best chronicler of Galveston.

Within a minute I was transported back to Galveston through Bill's picture words. Perhaps he is best known to many Galvestonians from his books, including *Bill Cherry's Galveston Memories,* which still brings Galveston alive through personalities, events and settings from the 1940s to present.

While there are several excellent history books on Galveston, none can animate Galveston like Bill's.

As the original owner of The House Company, still a large real estate firm, he saw it all. And he knew everyone from the very rich, to the famous, to the shoeshine boy. Through Bill's newspaper articles and books, I learned more about Galveston than I did from all the other books put together.

As a Born on the Islander (BOI), he watched, listened and processedthe world of deals, entertainments, and day-to-day activities in the port city. He clearly knows Galveston, past and present. And while he was a commercial real estate broker for 35 years, today he sees himself as a jazz pianist and author.

A few years ago, after writing columns for *The Galveston County Daily News,* the oldest newspaper in Texas, I asked the editor, Heber Taylor, to introduce us. After the introduction, I ventured a tentative email to Bill at world headquarters asking for a few minutes to visit him on my passage through the Dallas area. I received a very generous and friendly invitation. The afternoon flashed by. The shadows were growing long when we had to stop.

His weekly coffee visits with Heber Taylor are famous even today in Galveston. People gathered around to hear their friendly debates and sharing of inside information. Some even ended up in Bill's books.

Heber kept asking Bill to write a column on style. Bill continued to reflect back to Heber, asking him to write his view of what style was. You can find Bill's version of the elements of style in his book, *Bill Cherry's Galveston Memories* on page 123, as it appeared in The Daily News.

The moral of this column is to ask questions. I did and thus began a friendship with a frank and valuable mentor.

Thanks, Bill Cherry.

"Galveston! Oh, Galveston!"

"Galveston! Oh, Galveston!" When I tell someone that I am from Galveston they usually sort of sing the first three words, "Galveston, Oh Galveston." We Galvestonians have all heard the response, it gets old. That's all of the song they know. Maybe they recall Glen Campbell made the song famous.

I heard Glen Campbell sing another song which has stuck in my head for 65 years: *"Riding down the trail to Albuquerque, saddle bags all filled with beans and jerky, heading for K Circle B, the TV ranch for you and me, K Circle B in Albuquerque."*

Glen Campbell started his career with his uncle, Dick Bills, in Albuquerque (my hometown), having moved in 1952 from Billstown, Arkansas as a tenth-grade high school dropout.

After listening to him on the radio I "met" him through a used black-and-white TV provided by Grandpa. It sat in an honored corner in our living room at a 45° angle. Every Saturday morning my brothers and I gathered around to sing K Circle B and watch cowboy movies. Once I attended a live broadcast, but Glen was long gone. Campbell had expanded beyond his uncle's show. By 1960 Hollywood came calling. He loaded up his 1957 Chevy and left Albuquerque for fame and fortune.

In L.A., he played with Frank Sinatra, the Beach Boys and

other singers as a member of the studio recording group, the *Wrecking Crew.* After appearing on the *Smothers Brothers Show* he got his own TV show with an audience of 50 million.

Songs written by Oklahoma born songwriter, Jimmy Webb, were discovered by Campbell in the 60's. Webb wrote from *Galveston* to *Wichita Lineman*, to *MacArthur Park* and *By the Time I Get to Phoenix*, among scores of other hit songs, most sung by Glen Campbell's ballad-perfect voice. In Oklahoma, Webb's compositions were often cited by my writing professor, Dr. Tibbie Shades.

We just lost Glen Campbell after a courageous battle with Alzheimer's. The man went out with his family, humor, and a tour of the country documented by the film *I'll Be Me.* He never lost the music and the songs which touched so many of us.

Yesterday I visited the product of another creative genius, Ross Ward. Alzheimer's took him, too. In the cool mountains of New Mexico Ross created Tinkertown, a museum of miniature Western towns, circuses and artistic paintings. His ingenious works still bring smiles and "Hey, look at this!" from children of all ages. I met a guy visiting from Wisconsin who asked where I was from and I soon heard:

> "Galveston, oh, Galveston,
> I still hear your sea winds blowing;
> Galveston, oh, Galveston,
> I still hear your sea waves crashing,
> Still see her standing by the water
> Standing there, looking out to sea.
> Galveston, oh, Galveston, I am so afraid of dying."

The next time I hear "*Galveston, oh Galveston*" from a stranger I will be less irritated and remember the singing country boy from Arkansas who stirred so many emotions and illustrated how to face death.

Chapter 3 – Port Operations

White Sand with No Smell

The bright white sand like material rushes by carried by a black belt. Meeting a belt from the other direction, the "sand" disappears down a hole. Cranes race overhead. The place is fast, and loud. Golf carts dash about monster front loaders standing ready. So, this is the source of our abundant food supply. All the way from South America the "sand" is fertilizer on its way to farms and gardens all over the Midwest.

Looking down from on high, the crane operator waves to Ted O'Rourke and me before rushing the crane's cab back over the ship's hold. Much of the cargo ship's orange hull is out of the water, evidence that unloading is about over. The huge bucket hurries back toward us over a large steel box funnel. Opening it drops a ton of white pebbles 30 feet, which are whisked away on the conveyor belt.

The front loaders are strapped under the bucket, lifted over the side of the ship and lowered through the 40-foot square opening. Down in the hold of the ship, workers stab from nooks with spikes. The bulldozers push the remaining piles to the center for the bucket to pick up. Every crumb will be cleaned from this ship.

Mr. Reggie Clark, from several generations of African-American wharf workers, is the supervisor. He is also an expert at getting that last small amount off the deck and out of the ship. The ship will return to South America for another load, spic and span.

Ted shows me the route of the sparkling fertilizer. From where the two belts meet beside the ship, it drops down to a larger belt with fins, under the road and up, up to the top of the large metal building. The motion over the large rollers is fast, smooth and never ending. This operation is 24/7 almost 30 hours straight. Tied to the pier, the ship is not making money.

All along the enormous metal shed are railroad tracks. About eight dirty grey hopper cars sit on the tracks. Appearing to be parked, the cars are in fact slowly creeping under a funnel, where the pellets in a light white smoke fills each car. On top of the car is a very young appearing African-American man, Jordan Stoval, a line attached from his vest to an overhead beam. Slowly walking on the catwalk, he watches the car fill up. With a walkie-talkie he communicates with the locomotive operator and Jeremy Pruns in a shack next door to the railcars. When that car is full, Jeremy, calmly stroking his full ZZ Top beard, punches a few buttons, signaling the computer how much weight to put in the next car.

Directly above, the treadmill carries tons of the white stuff to drop in the next car. Using a calculator, Jeremy adds up the total load. This dangerous, intense and coordinated process goes on hour after hour.

These union longshoremen are focused and methodical. Glad I am retired. I might become bored and that could be deadly.

Port in full operation

What a Difference a Day Makes

We remember certain days. December 7, November 22, and 9/11. What happened on those dates changed lives. After the bombing of Pearl Harbor, men and women enlisted. With 9/11, Americans volunteered for military services and others to secure the U.S.

On 9/11, a new police academy graduate was manning a small booth on the Galveston wharf. Listening to local radio, he was unaware of the terrible tragedy occurring in New York as he checked trucks in and out of the port. Later that day he learned about the breakdown in U.S. security and the deadly results.

The newly formed Homeland Security identified U.S. ports as highly vulnerable targets, including Galveston. There was no fence, clearances or real security. I recall wandering the wharves close to ships and cargo.

Flash forward, 2015. Today I have a meeting scheduled with that same port police officer. So, on this beautiful spring day, I am looking for parking around Pier 25—good luck, even with no cruise ships in port. With a clamshell phone, I boycott parking meters. Driving by the front of the Shearn Moody building, I see a young man in civvies wearing a badge walk out. Using said phone, I call and ask him if he just walked out of the building. He answers yes and suggests I park in front of the Terminal. Parking problem solved.

We enter the Terminal One, Get Smart style, through multiple locked doors, on our way to his office. Housed in the world's largest passenger terminal with one berth, this is the center of Port Security. And the young (to me) man in charge is Brett Milutin. On 9/11 he saw his career begin with the process of securing the Port of Galveston. In 2011, he became the Facility Security Officer and Asst. Harbormaster.

So much goes on behind the scenes at the Port. Mountains of reports and studies are completed so the Wharves Board can inform everyone from the City Council to Feds in D. C. Brett coordinates with numerous agencies and shipping companies. He has grown up on the wharf, and it shows as we discuss the multitude of facets of operating the Port.

Passengers see only a small part of the security that keeps them safe from arrival until their ship is at sea. Detailed plans are in place in preparation for any possible event.

Ships are small towns at sea, and sometimes folks need to be locked up. Lt. Ostermayer explains that when suspects arrive back in Galveston, two cells welcome them until charges can be sorted out. If there are outstanding warrants in other states, the Port Police work on extradition.

Brett demonstrates how the nerve center helps keep us safe. TV cameras, screens and computers track ships and cargo—including human and cattle. A very busy place indeed.

On this date, I get the sense this is the right person for the job, at the right time.

Directing the Port of Galveston

What a view, eight stories above the Railroad Museum, the Port of Galveston looks like a model. One-thousand-foot long cruise ships line the wharves, along railroad rails, restaurants, up to the *Elissa*. Beyond are the Ocean Star, banana containers, and tractors. Sweeping right is the ship channel out to the Gulf of Mexico.

Turning my head as if at a tennis match, I look across at Pelican Island from Seawolf Park past tugboats waiting to bring in ships. Gulf Copper yard has ships under repair, and jack-up oilrigs taken apart. A bit further down is Texas A&M with the *General Rudder* tied up waiting for student mariners to go to sea.

Back on the Galveston side, a life size railroad yard, with a multitude of switches to more tracks. Long lines of oil and grain cars slowly move through the yard, horns sounding in the distance.

A smiling gentleman walks up and says, "quite a view," and I agree. Mike Mierzwa, the Port Director, ushers me into a corner working office, clearly not a meeting room. Stacks of paper are everywhere. They must be organized, as later my host easily retrieves a map to answer a question.

Just returned from a business trip, he is right on time to meet with this occasional columnist. A Born On the Islander—not Galveston, but Oahu, he completed a Coast Guard career in 1998, and has been at the Port 15 years, the past three as port director. His wife's family, the Williams, have run a fishing business from Pier 19 since 1946.

Over the next hour he answers all of my questions with an experienced encyclopedic memory demonstrating an insight of the intricate operation of the Port. Faster than I can write, he lists dimensions, costs, and numbers on details of the Port.

This place is a big business, with complex income and expenses. Trains are billed by the number of switches, cargo ships by the time and cargo across the wharf through a calculus formula, and cruise ships parking lots by number of trips. The Port is the fourth largest cruise ship port in the US, bringing over 600,000 passengers across the wharves each year. The size of warehouses, and the tonnage they hold all quickly come to my ears.

Neither one of us is a good sitter, often we arise, moving from wall maps to the windows as he explains what has been completed over the past 190 years and options for the future.

Making the right choices is critical to the Wharves Board, Galveston Island, County and beyond.

As we walk out, I feel valued to have had this time. Parting, we discover that both of our fathers served in the Navy during WWII on destroyers. We seem to have much more to discuss, though I may want to wait until his retirement—the Port needs his expertise now. See the Port of Galveston's website for wonderful pictures and information, including Wharves Board meetings.

Behind the Scenes with the Port Police

Sunday morning 7 a.m., standing in front of the Port of Galveston Police station, I glance over to see a large condominium like building glide by with folks on balconies enjoying the cool morning. It's the cruise ship *Navigator* docking right here at Pier 28.

I remember how a few weeks ago, Chief Pierce invited me to complete a ride-along application. Stopping by, just to drop off the forms on my way to work on USS *Stewart,* the receptionist saw my name and requested that I wait.

Soon Chief Pierce invited me in. What a contrast we were, he in a crease perfect uniform loaded with weapons, fit as could be and me in my painting clothes. Not a good impression. I apologized and he said, "No problem." Visiting and interviewing, while he read the application, began to remind me of my college oral exams. Looking me in the eye he stated he was approving me. Relief. Today, wakened from my daydream by Corporal Tamayo saying hello, I'm ushered into the squad room. I meet a diverse group including Officer Mike Washington, whom I will shadow today. A twelve-year African-American veteran, originally from Louisiana, he first worked at UTMB before attending the Academy.

Climbing up into the police van, we begin his shift cruising around the west sector. One of three sections, we check gates while making sure no one is hiding among wind towers, military personnel carriers, Airstream trailers or used cars waiting to be shipped out. This place is so much larger than it looks from Harborside Drive. One ship's crew is already busy welding a rail this morning. The Port never rests.

We approach a proud black bow; USS *Sturgis* is there right in front of me. Beautiful lines, with a cream colored modern super-structure. One of few Liberty ships left, her nuclear components are being removed at the Marlin shipyard. She looks like she could still sail the seas even after 75 years of service.

A call comes in regarding an arriving passenger with an outstanding warrant. They should not have gone on a cruise. Suspects soon meet a Port of Galveston Police Officer in a holding cell behind U.S. Customs. If the warrant is confirmed, port police transport the accused to the county jail. From there, they are transported to a facility by the jurisdiction where the alleged crime occurred.

Driving through the taxis, buses and trains, it's like sale day at a mall after Thanksgiving. Arriving passengers overlap with those rushing to board. Calls come in for contraband cases, mostly forgotten ammunition and weapons. After clearing a national record search, the passenger can have the police store their weapons if they are allowed to go on the cruise. That is up to the ship's captain. Often the answer is "no."

We arrive back at the office so Officer Washington can continue his day with paperwork. He says I am welcome to stick around. Quickly heading out the door I thank him, looking forward to the rest of my day away from the crowds and suspects.

Free Boat Tour of Port of Houston

My first impression of the Port of Houston at Allen's Landing, is what are they thinking? I could see the small Bayou from my office building at the University of Houston-Downtown. I think for years I wondered, how could this be one of the largest ports in the world? In retirement, I can satisfy my wonder and visit the Port. And am I glad Idid.

As Dee Dee knows, I am often on the Harbor boat tour in Galveston. Always amazed at how such large ships maneuver in the harbor and head down the channel to the Gulf, just around the corner.

In the non-mosquito season, I often go to the east end and watch the ships narrowly pass in the channel, not far from shore. Vandy Anderson has explained the critical role pilots play inkeeping ships in the channel. Knowing this, but not all of the story, I had quite a start, leaving on the *Triumph* last year.

As the *Triumph* left Galveston we rounded the east end, standing above the bridge, I noticed the bow moving a couple of points to port, which would soon have us out of the channel and grounded. Just as my heart began to rush, the captain announced on the loudspeaker that we were returning to the wharf because a passenger was having a heart attack. We did not hit anything.

Later in the voyage, I was able to thank the captain in person for telling us what he was doing. He patiently explained there is a turning basin just off the east end of the island. Oh.

The Houston ship channel is 52 miles long, including 25 miles in the Port of Houston. The channel is dredged to 45 feet deep and is only 530 feet wide, all the way from Houston past Galveston out to the Gulf. A big ditch in a bay, most of which is only 12 feet deep. Now consider some of the ships are 1,000 feet long and draw over 30 feet of water, including the *Triumph*.

The history of how Galveston became the little brother to the Port of Houston is a very interesting political and engineering story and not fully known. The Port of Houston just celebrated 100 years as a deep-water port. The same age as the Panama Canal. The Port of Houston stats are impressive. Largest U.S.A. port in terms of tonnage with over 8,000 ship and 200,000 barge visits per year. One million jobs in Texas supported by the Port and over $4.5B paid in taxes.

You can see the Port up close for free on the 100-foot *Sam Houston*, which sails each day. You must make a reservation (713 670-2416).

The *Sam Houston* motors by ships of all types. RO/RO (which roll off cars), cargo, tankers, bulk carriers, container, tugs, and barges are tied up along Buffalo Bayou, a narrow groove, not a large open area. A new fireboat showed off its large spray which reached almost across the channel.

The informative tour answered my port questions while providing an interesting, relaxing cruise.

Round the World Education Over Lunch

Nautical terms whiz by at a New-York-minute pace. Sitting in the back of Sonny's Place, an Island hamburger institution, Mike Leahy explains the ranks and privileges of US Navy, Merchant Marine, and Coast Guard personnel, all before the ice tea arrives. Each rank is illustrated with an example and moral of the story.

A few years ago, wanting to learn more about the wharves, I called a few ship repair companies. Mike called me back. Soon I was climbing the stairs to this astonishing seafarer's office.

Mike is the general manager of Malin International Inc., located on Pier 41 in Galveston. Here is an amazing complex of welding, milling and piping, all necessary for ship upgrades and maintenance.

Born in Bayonne, New Jersey, on the edge of New York City's harbor, next to the Statue of Liberty, the wharf is still Mike's home. Mike joined the United States Merchant Marine in 1971, during the Vietnam War. Beginning as an Ordinary Seaman, he rose through more challenging positions.

In the Merchant Marine, endorsements, similar to ranks, are related to time at sea and passing exams. After years at sea, Mike accumulated enough time to earn endorsements as fireman, watertender, oiler, deck engineer, chief pumpman and later first engineer.

As a civilian, he remained in the forefront of supporting military actions through service on board SS *Santa Anna*, delivering munitions for Operation Desert Storm—a critical job when the cargo includes bombs.

His work led to San Francisco as port engineer for a shipping company, and then as superintendent for MTL tankers on the West Coast in the early 1990's.

One day at lunch in a local diner Mike shared with his boss that his secretary, the only computer wise person in the office, was resigning. Computers were just beginning to be employed in the shipping business.

The waitress listened. When Mike finished, she said, "I know how to use computers, I could do the job." "Really?" Mike replied. "Can you come over this afternoon and see if you understand it?"

"Sure," she said. Long story short, Susan, last name now Leahy, went to work and met her husband of now 19 years. A wharf love story for sure. One day I mentioned to Susan how much I enjoyed conversing with Mike. "Why do you think I married him?" she asked.

Mike is a most interesting, broadminded, insightful gentleman. For instance, I told him my story of getting chewed out by a white attendant for mistakenly using the "colored" restroom in the south in 1964.

"In South Africa in the 1970's a black person would have been imprisoned for using the wrong restroom," Mike replied. He knows; he was there. Mike, a white man, and his African-American sailor friend, could not even ride in the same cab ashore without fear of incarceration.

After hours chatting with Mike, it is clear there is so much more to learn. More wharf stories I will continue to enjoy.

Master Wharf Puzzle Solver

My TWIC ID and a polite nod from the Port Police cleared me to drive among dozens of maneuvering 18-wheelers on the wharf. Where is the office? An SUV with a Master Gardener license plate answers my question.

Housed in the trailer on Pier 15, this is a center of conundrum solving. Susan Meads-Leahy is sitting behind a dark wood desk, with double monitors, used to decipher puzzles every day. A bright safety vest and construction hardhat hangs on the wall, ready for use.

On the desk is a large jar of seashells. Rare shells (wentletrap, baby's ear, tiger-eye) are just a few collected for a wreath for the Seafarer Center's gala. This woman always seems to have a purpose. Susan can answer shipping questions as well as how to cure gardening woes. Her understanding may stem from her itinerant life. From Mobile, to San Francisco, Hawaii, Galveston, South Carolina, New Orleans and back to Galveston. The common theme is the wharf. It's where she even found her husband.

Her experience has brought her to the position of Assistant Port Operations Director of Galveston's American Roll-On and Roll-Off Carriers (RO/RO). Located next to a large warehouse on the wharf, the office is the epicenter for the transfer of tons of cargo.

The most precious cargo to Susan are the boxes, which contain military family home items. Family photos, furniture, clothing, toys and other personal belongings, which can make living abroad protecting our freedoms a bit easier for families.

Susan has nine family members who served in the military so this is this is personal. What she does for other families is help facilitate their belongings arriving quickly in good condition. Other military assets, such as vehicles, are transported too.

Which leads to the computer screens where she and Robin, her boss, employ their logistical expertise. Susan is currently learning how to design a plan, a drawing, for where each cargo item—they aren't all nicely shaped boxes—will fit on each ship. Weight is critical and adds to the multitude of considerations, which must be addressed. When an item doesn't fit, she must redo the plan.

When freight arrives on trucks, she assures that it is all there and not damaged. If it is damaged, she tries to make it right. Each vessel is turned around in six to twelve hours.

In the processes, she interacts with as many as forty International Longshoremen, numerous truck drivers and crew members allowed off the ship. She is a master attitude adjuster.

The ship's crew occasionally find soft drinks in the office. They bring Susan and Robin chocolate from Germany. With so few women working on the wharf their motherly approach is most appreciated. Susan pulls out a photo album. "We will do our best to find this lost album's family," she said. "The least we can do is honor the families by getting them their belongings."

No doubt she will; she is a master puzzle solver.

Galveston's Seafarer Center—A Holiday Touch

Dusk has just passed. From Seawall and 45th I count 33 lights on the edge of the sea. Almost 2,300 souls aboard, waiting to come into port.

This holiday, 1.2 million seafarers are at sea, including 700,000 from the Philippines. Sailors live on the margins of society, mostly beyond the reach of land. It is a life of isolation away from families. Ships do not take holidays. Sailors are on a four-hour watch, off eight hours with some voyages lasting months.

Meanwhile on land, from Halloween to Christmas Eve, every store is packed with tons of potential gifts. Yet, the sailors who bring the presents thousands of miles, themselves often go without even one gift.

Not so in Galveston. One thousand sailors will receive a shoebox of gifts through the Galveston Seafarers Center. An additional 10,000 boxes will be given in Houston. As Rick Cousins wrote January 11, 2014, in the Daily News, Galveston is home of the remarkable Chaplain Karen Parsons, the driving force behind the shoeboxes.

Afraid of heights and water, this woman climbs 60 feet up on a swinging gangway up the side of ships in port to deliver gifts. Ships which were at anchor off Galveston.

One year on the "Banana boat" ship the crew of Ukraine and Russian sailors slowly, unwrapped their shoeboxes, careful not to tear the paper. After looking at the gifts of personal items, drawings by children and postcards, they rewrapped the boxes, still in awe. When asked why, they said they wanted their families to experience opening the present too. They could not believe that strangers would give them presents.

Another Christmas, a ship caught fire and two sailors died. The crew was mostly from the Philippines. While the investigation went on aboard ship, the crew was housed at the La Quinta on the seawall. They grieved the loss of their friends. Crewmembers were allowed to dine at Denny's, but their main staple, rice, was not on the menu. Chaplain Parsons to the rescue, or should I say kitchen?

Less than 2% of sailors on merchant ships are women, and about 18% on cruise ships. Sexual harassment is a major problem for women who work in regular seafarer jobs. One woman in the engineering department shaved her head and dressed as a man to protect herself.

One study indicates the presence of women on the crew reduces the feelings of isolation and thus could reduce crew turnover. The main reason given for seamen not shipping out again is to be with family.

Four local stores later, and with an aching back I finish putting together five plastic shoeboxes. Included are postcards, holiday towels, personal items, Santa hats and hand-written cards wishing seafarers a peaceful holiday season. How do Chaplain Parsons and Melissa produce 1,000? To help, see the Center's website and scroll to Santa for Seafarers. You'll appreciate and feel closer to the many sailors off our shore.

www.galvestonseafarer center.org.

Crew of Pan Viva: Chaplain Karen Parsons center, Kathy Sallee to right and author standing to left

Christmas Gifts on a Slow Ship to China

Standing on Pier 32/33, staring up, the cargo ship looks huge. Fresh paint to the waterline mark is still fifteen feet out of water. The ship is just beginning to fill up with ball-bearing shaped Texas soybeans showering from above into the large hole.

Climbing four stories up aluminum stairs, slick from soybean dust we step on the main deck. Gasp. We are greeted with smiles and tags to wear. Then back down with two seafarers to fetch holiday wrapped shoeboxes full of goodies. Back up the gangway. Following with the plate of fudge, I slip a bit. Close call. Gasp.

Walking aft, we enter a slight skyscraper, up more stairs to a small bleak recreation room. Gasp. Feeling closed in, I peek out a porthole toward the long ship's bow and the cruise ship *Triumph*. What a contrast. The *Pan Viva* is almost the length of a cruise ship, but this is a no-frills bulk carrier. Today's version of the *Elissa*. Based in Korea, it "carries your dreams" (actually Texas farmers' dreams) and is "a most admired company." Just the same I'll take the *Triumph*. The second mate explains that it will take fifty-five nonstop days to arrive in

China. No Wi-Fi. The crew of seventeen Filipino men and five Korean officers will be at sea on Christmas. Having just sailed from Turkey most have contracts through next June before they can return home.

We are here with Chaplain Karen Parsons, OFS of the Seafarers Center. Last year I wrote of my effort of five shoeboxes filled with socks to playing cards. As this year's 22 boxes are stacked on the table, more young men drift in. Shy at first, they light up when homemade fudge is offered. Cellphone cameras come out and soon the group is cutting up, just like with my brothers during photo ops. This is a group of entertainers, for sure.

Chaplain Parsons asks how they are doing using general open-ended questions. All seems good. She inquires if they would like a communion service later. That evening with one wife joining through Skype, they celebrate with joy.

Twenty-two souls, fifty-five days on a utilitarian ship, hard work, away from family. Hopefully the Galveston gifts will make one day a bit special, as it did for me today.

Free Ferry Ride is on Me

Not often do I drive the car off the wharf. Once I rode my bicycle off of a diving board, ouch. So far, the ferry has always been at the wharf. A deck hand in a yellow vest directs us to our spot, hopefully outside, front row.

When our kids were young, I acted like I was driving the ferry with the car's steering wheel. Of course, when they got older they caught on. Now I am trying the same thing with our granddaughters. 8-year-old Nicole is on to me, while 3-year-old Violet still believes Papa drives the boat. Many of us are still kids at heart when we head out on the ferry ride.

Once underway we pile out of the car and head to the bow or stern to view the sights. The scenery is wonderful. Dolphins frolic, ships steam past as gulls swarm over the rail. Heading upstairs for an even better view and the restrooms, we meet a gentleman wearing a bike helmet. He rides his bike while his wife drive. Later, on Bolivar, he is walking with a flat. Best laid plans.

On one mid-morning ferry ride, the traffic line is so long I decide to walk on. In the waiting area, you watch the TXDOT men and women guide cars and trucks on board. Walk-ons are last. The ramp comes up and off we go, white foam bubbling up behind the ferry.

"Why all the traffic? I ask David, a deckhand. "Cruise ship day," he says. A BOI, he got on with the ferry four years ago after doing *Ike* construction. He wishes people wouldn't get out of their cars during loading. A few car doors have been lost that way. Some drivers try to change lanes. Center lanes are larger for trucks. It's all a giant puzzle, one David knows how to solve, every twenty minutes.

A couple in a large motor home tells me they got the front row by tipping. Ha. They are from Nevada on their way to Florida and then DC. After Galveston, they have only four states left to visit.

As a walk on, I stay on the ferry upstairs as cars and trucks roar off and on--a controlled traffic jam. Looking down, I notice the RV has a good roof, the mail truck a clear roof and the semi is missing part of the rooftop—interesting perspective. Glancing up at the walkway above I see a confident woman stride to the bow wheelhouse. I asked David if she is the captain. "No," he says, "she's an AB," meaning Able Body Seaman, rated to steer the ferry along with the captain.

As we return to Galveston, five young women come downstairs, wearing "ship face" shirts—yes, it is a fun cruise ship day in the middle of this important highway. The ferry is both a hurricane disaster route and a pleasant free ride.

A Bridge to Nowhere, is Now to Somewhere

Unaware, we often travel right over a major interstate. The Intracoastal Waterway runs 3,000 miles through the Port of Galveston under I-45 and the Pelican Island Bridge. I am on my way to investigate. Barely surviving 51st and Broadway, I am amazed anyone with a straight face can call the median historical—maybe for carriages. If the intersection is corrected, it might be historical.

The Pelican Island Bridge is considered an historical bascule-type draw bridge. Designed by A&M engineers and built in 1957 for $7M. Wait, that's younger than me. Back then there wasn't much on Pelican Island. No Texas A&M-Galveston or industry, only the shipyard, served by a ferry. The Island was still being constructed with spoil from dredging the ship channels.

The first business to open on the island was KGBC radio station in 1958. Their "Keeping Galveston Beaches Clean" (KGBC) jingle is still a good idea, according to my neighbor, Big Rey Soto of the Parks Department. The radio staff included a young DJ, Capt. Vandy Anderson, now the Chair of Navigation District One Commission. Among other duties they oversee the bridge. I am off to meet an employee, David Flores. That is if I can get through the honking and swearing on Broadway.

Parking in the bridge's two-car parking lot, I knock on the wooden screen door. A burly gray-haired gentleman opens the door welcoming me with a big voice. Eager, he begins the tour without even one question from me. A tug radios in and David Flores replies in English, but I don't understand one word of the sea-going jargon.

Standing in command behind the large 1950's control panel, he explains each move, checking traffic, sounding the siren, gates, down, and barrier swings over. Then clutch in, shift to first gear raising the 31-foot wide, 195-foot long rated span almost straight up. The tug, one of hundreds, passes with a honk. The process is reversed and an entry made in the logbook—even old bridges have bureaucracy.

David came to work here 26 years ago from shipping, handy, as the bridge is run by ship engines. He keeps telling me it is simple. Okay, maybe for him with extensive experience. Not for me. "Do you want to see under the bridge?" David asks. He opens the cover to the stairwell, which goes down, down to an open 80-foot pit. The greased huge rocker arm is out of the industrial revolution.

Scary. Heading into more dangerous territory, David asks if I want to continue. "Okay," I answer, before thinking. We end up on a two-foot wide catwalk down next to the water rushing out fast with the current.

We visit some more; he is proud to be part of the Port and sees great potential. Then sounding the siren, stopping traffic he allows me to back my car out. I respond with a honk, thankful, as I head home, for the bridge and skilled operators.

Pulling in the driveway my knees begin shaking, a delayed reaction to my thrilling exploring. Which is still easy for David Flores.

A Magic Parking Job

It's a turtleneck, long-sleeve T-shirt morning on Wharf 21. The north wind creates a cold AC effect. Already 7:30 AM and no ships at Pier 25? Strange. No fog. What gives? Gazing down the channel to USS *Stewart*, I see a new skyscraper. Oh, it is the cruise ship *Magic*. Barely moving the beautiful white ship approaches the Yacht Club.

Flags blowing straight out, small sticks rushing by the dock at a current of about three knots (3.5 mph); this is not going to be an easy day to dock. The *Magic* is 1,004 feet long, about 15 stories tall, with a 158-foot beam (width).

The pilot, according to definition, must calculate "the ship's silhouette data (i.e. windage and lateral plane data) for a given load (i.e. displacement and centre of gravity) for a ship's equilibrium floatation for a free or 0° heel angle." (Keep in mind that no equilibrium can be found when transverse/ longitudinal GM is negative or displacement exceeds ship's buoyancy.)

If you are still reading, I promise no more formulas. Yes, there are computer programs to figure this out. Yet, it is the pilot who must translate all of this information to action. The ship is going to move, no matter if the propellers stop. The bow will move leeward even dead in the water.

Slowly the bow turns toward the Yacht Club and keeps going. A mistake? No, the *Magic* needs to back in, so reversing in the new turning basin is normal, except now there is windage and the current running out.

The dogs and I wander down the wharf to the end of Terminal One. Craning my neck, I look up as the ship, containing a city, eases to the dock touching the bumpers without even a tap that would wake a baby.

A pilot boat motors up, ramming up against the pier just in front of us. In the background the *Triumph*—another cruise ship—bow first, slips past us. Wow. A well-balanced act in tight quarters, for sure.

Soon the pilot walks down the wharf and steps on the bow platform on the pilot boat. Yelling "Good Morning," he waves back. "Smooth backing up and docking on a bad day," I holler. He answers, "Oh, I just brought it to the basin and the captain docked."

Just as expected, modest, calm and in the background, pilots work as silent servants protecting the public. They pilot all kinds of ships 24/7. Unmistakably skilled and experienced in safely guiding huge ships with over 4,000 crew and passengers through a narrow channel on a turtleneck day, for Galveston-Texas city pilots, it's not magic, it's their job.

Ladders to Success: Pilots in Galveston

Early in the morning a dense fog bank lies between the jetties. Semi-trucks, buses alongside cabs idle at the wharf. Cruise ship passengers prepare to disembark. On shore, others can't wait to create Caribbean memories. For the ballet to begin the fog curtain must lift.

Just off shore, eight decks above the sea, the captain explains to the pilot all of the technology available to "see" through the fog. He points out that the fog bank is narrow. Time is ticking. The pilot agrees technology is an aide; he has his own computer and data.

Yet, the pilot suggests stopping the ship. The captain commands, "All stop ahead." Fifteen minutes pass, the fog clears and the massive ship comes back to speed. Using the tool of situational awareness, the pilot gazes off to the starboard, and sees two small shapes passing out of the channel. The shapes are two kayakers. Minutes before they were in the channel right in front of the 130,000-ton ship.

They owe their lives to the Galveston-Texas City pilot—the umpire—who makes correct decisions for 5,000 ship relocations per year. Making calls like, going full speed ahead, while turning the opposite direction the ship needs to go, takes experience and supreme confidence. And knowing the current ends as soon as you clear the point.

While pilots bring in cruise ships weekly, most of the ships they pilot are bulk carriers, tankers and occasionally oilrigs. Boarding these ships at the sea buoy, about twelve miles from port is challenging and sometimes heart-stopping. When boarding a cruise ship, the pilot basically steps from a tossing pilot boat across a few feet into a large open door. The challenge is trying to keep anyone from "helping" which might affect the pilot's balance.

Cargo ships are another matter. You can see them from Fort Point, appearing often as large rust buckets to me. To the pilot what matters is the ladder condition up the freeboard. The distance from the deck down to the water is between 30 and 50 feet, depending on whether the ship is loaded.

The pilot climbs a Jacob's ladder, ropes with wood or rubber rungs, all the way from the water to the deck. To get a sense, go to the Stewart Title building on 22nd. Stand right next to the wall and look straight up past the arches to the capstone. That is about 50 feet. Add a swinging ladder above waves in the dark, climb hand over hand all the way up. Now you begin your day at the office.

The ladders are not always in good shape. One side broke half way up, pinning Pilot Derek Tracy's feet to the other side. The ship's crew was not paying attention. He reached high up on one side and freed himself, almost falling back into the ocean. Want to make the big bucks? Neither do I.

Chapter 4 - Personalities

Dee Dee Welcomes the World on Pier 22

Once in a while in our hectic lives there is an oasis. Things are just right. Some sunny afternoon, stand at the door of the Texas Seaport Museum gift shop. With questions on their faces, hundreds of folks walk through the door at the end of Pier 22. They wonder about the beautiful sailing ship. They wonder about planning an event, touring the museum, where the best place is to eat and a harbor tour. Oh, and they wonder where the bathrooms are.

Behind the counter in this whirlwind is a middle-aged, thin, friendly-natured woman, graying hair pulled back in ponytail. Calm and polite as she answers all of the questions—after all, this is the South. Immediately you sense her competence and strength.

Dee Dee McCandless is the first person many of us meet at the wharf. Engaging folks even before they awkwardly ask questions is her signature. Her philosophy is to open up to people, then they open up to her. Conversing, they buy more.

The gift shop is really the center of the world. In a few minutes Australians, Brits and Midwesterners pass through discussing Panama, Steve Irwin, and California.

Recently, hosting two Vancouver couples, we went to Fisherman's Wharf. With a great view of the *Elissa*, we saw a high school Navy ROTC group of about 30 young people come up from below deck and head out on the Seagull II for a harbor tour. Soon a light mist turned to real rain. Of course, my New Mexico umbrella turned inside out with the first gush of wind. We all made it to the Seaport Museum backdoor. Someone (Dee

Dee) had unlocked the "Do Not Enter" door. I ushered the polite Canadians inside. Making our way to pay we are met by Dee Dee with rolls of paper towels. Crisis addressed.

Just as I was inquiring how she knew we were coming, the thirty ROTC students came in the front door soaked to the bone. They quickly organize themselves as Dee Dee directed them, with omnipresent paper towels, to the large bathrooms with tiled floors. In five minutes, you had no idea a disaster had just passed through the gift shop.

A mother and adoptive mom of five homeschooled, now grown, men, Dee Dee and her family fish at every chance. Or should I say, catch? Including a 42" redfish.

She first visited Galveston as a child. Thirty years ago, on a vacation to Galveston with her husband, Darrell, they decided to move from Dallas (I could say something here). Four days later, she was waiting tables at Miller's and until *Ike*, at Seahorse Lanes. Four years ago, her dream job on the wharf became reality—meeting, greeting, explaining and calming brides to be. (Ask to see the high heel gauge.)

Her love of the sea and history is clear in her smile and answers to every question. In my view, she is the perfect person to welcome the world to Galveston's wharves.

Fishing Family Flourishes with Friends in Island Life

It was 6 a.m. when Henry Homrighaus, 73, of Texas City and I walked down the Galveston Yacht Basin wharf looking for the *Loan Shark*, Capt. Shawn Warren's boat. Soon, with Warren's 9-year-old son, Buck, as first mate, we prepared for a friendly fishing competition. "Growing up, I was always competitive, playing every sport, until everyone was bigger," Capt. Shawn said laughing. "Fishing met that need."

His first photo at age two was with a fishing rod and fish. Competition began at age 19 when he won a new Z71 pickup and a 22-foot boat, motor and trailer. Competitiveness continued in his business career as a residential loan officer.

Entertaining clients on fishing trips was a natural—his experience always had them catching. The market crashed just as Capt. Shawn became a full-time father.

Captain Shawn and Buck aboard The Loan Shark

"It was important to raise my son on the island, spending time with him," he said. "My dad was gone for six months at a time working in the oil fields. When dad was home, we fished together, but when he had to leave, it was hard on us. I didn't want that for my son."

Capt. Shawn Warren has a six-pack captain's license—he can take up to six anglers at a time. Customers tell him which fish they desire and he takes care of everything else. His website shows everything from tarpon to sharks, along with enormous angler smiles. Buck is a precocious Huck Finn with haircut to match. A fourth-grader at Holy Family Catholic School, his education was early and extra. He was writing cursive in second grade.

The family's Galveston history is deep—grandparents graduated from the University of Texas Medical Branch and a great-uncle was Cardinal Bernard Ganter.

On calm waters, the boat streaked down the channel, rounded the South Jetty on an incoming tide, which rippled the water, resembling a river. Capt. Shawn, the true athlete, quickly moved about the rocking boat, dropping anchor and baiting rods.

A skilled fisherman, Homrighaus's first cast hit immediately. He repeated the process several times. Capt. Shawn set a pole for me, as I said, "I am not fishing, just writing." Three seconds later, a fish hit and he handed the pole to me. Dropping my notebook I ran forward, keeping the line from the props. Buck, like a gymnast, grabbed the net and leaned over the side as I plopped the sizeable fish into the net. Buck swung the fish on deck, pulled the hook and measured, thirty-two inches.

"Thirty-two inches—too big." He said. After a quick photo, overboard it went. "What?" I cried out, now engaged in this sport. "It was the largest."

"Redfish between 20 and 28 inches are keepers," said Capt. Shawn. Conversant with regulations, the sea, its creatures, weather and boats, the Captain knows.

We settled into a routine on the quiet sea. "Can we practice knots instead of playing with the iPad when we get home?" Buck asked.

"Sure Buckaroo," his dad answered.

While I write, Homrighaus and Buck hooked fish after fish and soon had five keepers. Buck wanted one more, so his father motored to a special spot with an eddy. "Last cast is the best," Buck yelled.

But not today. The best was that evening when the triad met at Cajun Greek Seafood, 2226 61st Street in Galveston. With owner Ilan Amsalem we feasted on fresh grilled and blackened redfish as fish tales were told. As Amsalem took Buck off to visit other diners, Capt. Shawn leaned back and smiled. "A perfect day with family and friends," he said. For more information for a fun filled charter, visit galvestonfishcommander.com

Note: Sadly, Henry Homrighaus, my good friend, suddenly passed Easter Morning dressed in his suit, ready to go to church and brunch at the Galvez Hotel with his fiancée, Grace.

Buck, author, and Henry Homrighaus (Photo by Capt. Shawn)

Capt. Wes of the *Seagull II*

My head down against a whitecaps-in-the-harbor cold wind, I shuffled out to Wharf 22. Darn, the door's locked. I am freezing. Time to learn the Belizean national anthem and move further south?

Capt. Wes Hocott strolled up wearing a light warm-up suit, and flip-flops. My eyes widen, but I didn't say anything. We went upstairs to the conference room. What a view. The bow of the cruise ship *Triumph* appeared to come through the side window. The harbor is spectacular.

How Capt. Wes came to have an office on the end of Wharf 22 wearing flip-flops is not what most would expect. True, his grandfather, whom he never met, served on a tin can (destroyer) off Galveston during WWII looking for U-boats. Yet the answer is not clear.

My quest is to follow up on some interesting stories Capt. Wes began but did not have time to finish during some of our harbor cruises on the *Seagull II*. Clearly my assumption (yes, I know, don't ...) of why someone would be a ship captain does not fit here.

Capt. Wes is the lead captain for the *Seagull II* and the Director of the Galveston Island Tours for the Galveston Historical Foundation. Sounds like a bureaucrat, but Capt. Wes is far from it.

I always thought being a captain would be everyone's dream. Yet, it's like my cousin who piloted 100 missions off an aircraft carrier in Viet Nam, not wanting to become an airline pilot. As a high school student, I couldn't understand why instead he wanted a master's degree in math.

Capt. Wes always does what makes him happy, which is helping others enjoy life more. He worked with after school programs for kids in Houston, and Club Med in Turks. He wanted to work at Club Med Cuba, way before the new travel policy. After working on Roatan, guiding excursions such as snorkeling and kayak tours, he came back to Clearlake. As a waiter on the Star Fleet Yacht he quickly worked his way up to supervisor. The captain interacted with passengers and Wes wanted that too. So off he went to get a captain's license.

Capt. Wes wanted more people interaction, and the *Seagull II* provided that. His delivery of the "script" is always fresh and if requested, he does the best ghost story when passing UTMB. He really engages kids (of all ages). Kids get to "drive" the boat on the way back to the dock. Parents (and grandparents) proudly take pictures and email them off around the world.

Of all the wonderful people our granddaughter Nicole has met on the island, Capt. Wes is the favorite guy. Dolphin and shark sightings may have something to do with it, but mostly it's his gift with children. So what about the flip-flops in cold weather? He got used tobare feet in Roatan, and he doesn't like shoes. As I walk away down the wharf, he yells after me, "Make me look good." No problem, Captain, you put a smile on our faces every time.

Do I Need a Duck License?

Wanted: Drivers for the Galveston Duck Boat Tours. Wow! This could be my dream job, wheeling a 6.5-ton, huge craft through Galveston traffic, while explaining the history of the grand ole town to attentive tourists. Well maybe not. First of all, George beat me to it 14 years ago. And he is something very special.

For many summers now, a favorite occasion for me is stopping at a red light—hey, tourists stop at green sometimes, and not at all at red. From high above in the yellow duck truck, I hear George's voice booming out interesting historical and current stories about our seaport town. The voice is full of energy, excitement and delight—every trip seems like his first. These are his best friends and he wants us to understand the who, what, where and why of Galveston. Always fresh and so engaging. I wave or yell "Hi," and he calmly waves back not missing abeat.

After reviewing the job requirements, I realize there is much more to George than I imagined. He has a Captain's and commercial driver'slicense,both required to give tours. Not to mention knowing how to drive a DUKW, a complex link to WWII including the invasion of Normandy. The initials are bureaucratese for a RV size jeep, which can drive at 55 MPH—good luck in the summer traffic on Galveston—and a seaworthy boat, which cruises at 6.4mph. All while negotiating a complex transmission. And it was the first vehicle where you could adjust tire pressure from inside the cab, a necessity on beaches. Galveston Duck boats began their service in 1998.

After a safety briefing, a wonderful blend of seriousness and humor, George drives east from 25th and Seawall. He hangs a U-turn on the way to 6lst Street and into Offatts Bayou for a jumping fish boat tour. Up the ramp and off to the Strand and the wharves, for more sights and sounds. A round-trip of fifteen miles, up to seven times a day.

What intrigues me about George is how he comes to the same job day after day and makes it appear as if he just started? With basic flash card information, he blends a custom story, for each trip to fit his audience. Less history for families with children, more for us mature folks. Just walking through the duck, he reads the group so well.

A master of multitasking, George, gauges the traffic lights just right, points out sights, and never says "ah," all while maneuvering through texting, tourist traffic. He provides pointers such as no glass on the beach, seawall parking, great restaurants, spots to explore and much more. He is the chamber of commerce, tourist bureau, Historic Foundation, community policeman, and comedian all rolled into one.

Whether you are a BOI, IBC or one-day tourist, George serves as another wonderful Galveston treasure, right here at the Pleasure Pier. It's summer, so I'm looking forward to some red stoplights so I can enjoy eavesdropping for a few moments. http://www.galvestonducks.com

Port Police Chief Pierce

As I began to get to know the wharves a few years ago when I began writing columns I soon learned the major role the Port of Galveston Police play in the Port's operation. To learn more, I knew I needed permission to ride along with the police from the chief. Some folks had told me the "chief" really liked the columns. I dropped by the station in my painting clothes just to turn in the form on my way to USS *Stewart* when the Chief asked to see me.

Chief Robert Pierce, in his perfect fitting creased uniform loaded with weapons, treated me with formal respect. We were and still are a real contrast. Yet with several lunches at Galveston's Happy Coffee Shop over Randy Abramson's creative cuisine of her native Cambodia, we became good friends. Our trails to this point are as varied as the high desert and the Gulf Coast.

Both of us were born in the shadow of the WWII greatest generation. The chief's father and mother were married in Abilene before his Dad hit the beaches and was wounded right after D-Day while serving in the U.S. Army.

Returning after the war, his father and mother had nine

children. Make that plus 129 foster children. Some of the kids became attached to the Pierce family for life.

After high school, Chief Pierce joined the Army, where he served a very busy ten years. He sums up the decision of his life as, "I learned and taught firearms, became a paratrooper, jumped into Korea on an exercise, humped the jungles and swamps during three posts in more than one foreign country, visited southeast Asia for a couple of years and received a college degree."

After his retirement from the Army he began seeking a career in law enforcement. He sent out 250 letters across the country.

"Fortunately, I took the first job offered and settled in Galveston, intending to stay two to three years, learn all there was to know about modern police service, and then head back up to the middle of South Dakota. Join the police, settle down, raise my family and run for sheriff."

As many of us know, Galveston has a way of not letting go. Fast forward 29 years later, after completing almost every assignment in the Galveston Police Department, including Chief of Police, he retired, thinking he was a dinosaur. But not for long.

Off he went to the Port Police force for twelve years, and soon was chief. Why not retirement I wonder?

He answers, "I am able to contribute to the well-being of our island community by facilitating commerce activities on the waterfront, maintaining order and security in a maritime environment, and guiding our visitors and friends as they pass through the facilities when the cruise ships arrive."

It has not been lost on me that this man, who oversees policing on the wharves, has "pier" as part of his name.

We finish another wonderful meal. Chief Pierce leans back and gently slaps his bulletproof vest, smiling and utters, "Ah, life is good."

Note: Chief Pierce retired last year. Last time I saw him, he had on shorts.

A Brief Conversation with Arlo Guthrie

If this island did not exist, there wouldn't be the best Port on the Gulf coast. No Port, then no wharves and no booming Strand in the 1800's. No wharves, no shipment of cotton, grain or immigration. Without this wealth, no Grand 1894 Opera House. And without the assistance of hundreds of folks, no restored, beautiful, historical venue today.

Without the wharves over the past one hundred-plus years, never an opportunity to obtain a last-minute standing room only ticket-orchestra level, A1 at that, to celebrate fifty years of Arlo Guthrie.

Our family paths crossed many times over the past century, but we had never met face to face. Dust bowl and depression lead our families from Oklahoma to the land of milk and honey in California. Family members went to sea during World War II. Arlo's father was a Merchant Mariner, "drunk once, sunk twice" in the North Sea, and mined in the South Pacific.

In the 1960s Arlo rode his motorcycle in Massachusetts (he wrote the state song) and I ran the Boston Marathon. Arlo flew to Woodstock in a helicopter; I watched the movie. He plays five guitars and the piano; I played the hi-fi record player, listening to a 33-RPM recording of the *Massacre*.

We both protested the Viet Nam War and were sad to lose our drafted friends and family, both through death and PTSD. We traveled on *The City of New Orleans* changing cars in Memphis, Tennessee. We flew, "*Coming into Los Angeles*" and traveled from California to the New York island. The Chinese, he pointed out, may have traveled the long way around.

During intermission, I looked out the window, and commented to Bujo, the usher, that the fog was denser. That morning on the beach, it reminded me of Cape Cod. He replied now it looked like San Francisco.

Like folks in Alaska, Galvestonians have interesting life scripts. Bujo began reminiscing about a bicycle trip from a small cabin on the *Queen Mary* in Long Beach to Ghirardelli's Chocolate Factory on the Bay. Meeting an articulate homeless man, Bujo learned a poor man's itinerary of San Francisco. We were doing a lot of life story telling this night.

Back to Alice's Restaurant and Woody Guthrie's never recorded words to live by. Arlo invited us to sing along. In her intro, Maureen Patton, the Executive Director, had asked us not to sing along, so we hesitated. Arlo encouraged us (he clearly had never heard me sing) and off we went on a loud sing along. It was a special moment for us. One encore and off he went.

Filing out, I turned east to find my car in the fog. As I passed the stage door, Arlo was getting on his bus. In a firm deep voice, I called out, "Arlo, thank you!" He turned slightly, waving shyly, with a genuine smile and said, "Thank you." Off stage, still a reluctant 19-year-old celebrity.

Looking for my car in the fog at the Trolley stop

Oleanders, Cruise and Cousins

From deck ten, just over the polished mahogany rail, the deep blue waters are touched by whitecaps under perfect shades of white clouds. Only a week and 2,000 miles ago I was in the Moody Gardens ninth floor Terrace Room overlooking the Bay and the Gulf. Images of Jean Lafitte and beautiful oleander flowers gently clicked by on the screen. The 50th

Anniversary of the International Oleander Society luncheon was about to begin.

A few months earlier my friend, board member Henry Homrighaus, had invited me to the celebration and wondered if he could suggest me as the keynote speaker. After a few weeks of hemming I explained my only knowledge of the Island flower was that I had watered them at a sorority when I was in high school. I finally said okay if they couldn't get someone better. A few days later Henry let me know they had found a fellow who sang sailor shanties. "Great," I responded.

When Henry finished his other pre-luncheon duties he sat next to me as the Jean Lafitte image reappeared. Over full-of-flavor gazpacho, I told Henry I had just finished reading William Davis' three-inch-thick book on the Lafitte brothers. I revealed the real truth of their years on Galveston proudly setting the record straight. More slides of oleander blooms rotated on the screen as the keynote speaker was introduced.

Much to my joy the speaker was Dr. Stephen Curley of Texas A&M- Galveston, whose writing (the "*Texas Clipper*" for one) I had admired for ten years, but had never met. The audience was treated to a series of fun stories of oleanders and Lafitte's pirate songs. One tune had been stolen from Woody Guthrie, who'd taken it from someone else. How fitting a pirated song about a pirate, Dr. Curley added. After a short account of how the oleander came to Galveston 175 years ago, Dr. Curley sang an encore. Not bad for a lit prof. I left with an autographed book, happy and relieved as I set off to board the cruise ship for Key West and points east.

At the last breakfast on the ship I met two new couples, both who had ties to Galveston. One a Ball High grad and the other a BOI. I asked Will, the BOI, what his last name was. He replied, "Homrighaus." I said, "So how are you related to Henry?" His eyes lit up. Henry was an older cousin, and he commenced with numerous yarns of Henry in his early days.

Henry knows much more than I ever will about Galveston, but now with emails set to come in from cousin Will, things may level out a bit. And now I know Henry's nickname. Come to think of it I know Henry well enough that I probably will still know less. One thing I do know once again: it's a small world after all.

A Tale of Two Tours: Part I: Key West's Denison

Elegant, eccentric, expensive, chic casas splashed with Caribbean colors layered in lush green. A veil of coconut tanning oil shimmers in the sunny morning still. An easy going Caribbean calm as the Atlantic greets the Gulf of Mexico.

Ah, relaxed Key West. Home to the Conch Republic, with their own tolerant thoughts. Smooth on the surface for tourists, turbulent tussled politics for the locals.

Narrow closed in cobblestoned paths crisscross the small island town. Duval, the main drag for one mile.

Key West has met me twice in the past year, in the form of Denison Tempel. His wharf-side greeting says it all—the best of Key West.

Tall, slim, and pale. Shorts, a turquoise shirt, collar pulled up, bandana about his neck. A fit 18-year-old up to his chin, the large joker's 70-year-old smile below mischievous dancing eyes reveals his true age. A casual silver haircut and rakish British driver's cap tops him off. Every pore breathes welcome to my comfortable island.

Gathering his dozen tourists, off we trek to the bike shop, pausing on each corner to hear a tale or two. The Post Office Custom House built in 1891, was the site for the inquiry into the sinking of USS *Maine* in Havana Harbor in 1898. Mel Fischer's shipwreck Treasure Museum and the Audubon House are just across the street.

Around the corner is Mallory Square, home of famous sunset celebrations. Tucked in Mallory's fame, at the original waters' edge, is a small overlooked Memorial Sculpture Garden. Busts of thirty-one influential local people accent the tropical floral peaceful garden with plaques explaining each contribution. Maybe another project for Galveston's historical Strand?

Turning into an alley we meet our bikes. Wearing a helmet, you are insured. Without, you're not. I am the only helmeted one.

Six miles go by, sights a-many, and with satisfaction we dismount wiser. Denison has carefully guided us through history, architecture and traffic in a gentle yet firm manner. Every question answered, wrapped in neat paragraphs, thirty-five years in the making.

Denison arrived in Florida in 1979 after an eight-hour plane ride from the United Kingdom where he studied architecture. Renting a car, he drove 150 miles south mostly on a narrow two lane elevated road on, for him, the wrong side of the road. He was exhausted. The next day as he explored the island of Key West, he never felt more at home.

He soon opened a bed and breakfast on Eaton Street. In later years, he served as the curator of the Donkey Milk House, circa 1866.

Retired, he now leads educational bike tours four times a week for cruise ship passengers. A dozen tourists are glad he does.

PostScript: The next year on another cruise, after becoming email pen pals, I visited Denison briefly on the wharf again. This time he wore a pith helmet. We jammed an hour's worth of conversation into twenty minutes. Next time, I may need to take a slow sailboat to Key West so we can visit for a few days.

A Tale of Two Tours: Part II Freeport's Leroy

Leroy of Freeport folds ten of us into his van and hops in the right-hand seat exclaiming, "Good morning, Mon!" Donny, a new, New Mexico friend and I are headed off for another bicycle tour.

Leroy points out sights while sharing Bahamas's backdrop. The island is 97 miles long by seven miles wide. A canal cuts through saving a 57-mile boat trip to the other side.

Freeport, the main city, was founded in 1955. Leroy adds that his entire 29 years have been on Grand Bahama, thus his dark tan. He is the only black person in the van.

On our bikes we are off at a fast clip, a couple of miles between stops. Under a plum tree Leroy asks, "Who is Columbus?" What is the answer? He "rediscovered" the Bahamas and brought death by sword and disease. October 12th here is National Heroes Day, not Columbus Day.

He focuses on each of us, person by person, often stepping into our personal space looking up from his wiry 5'6" frame, black eyes fixed on ours earnestly sharing his history and his story. He is a truly excellent teacher, weaving facts through storytelling.

During a break, I encourage him to go into education, "Kids will remember your lessons, tourists will soon forget," I philosophize.

Looking up at me, he reflects, "I have thought about that," and then trails off. College education is a challenge out here. Seventy percent of the economy comes from tourists, so that's where the jobs are.

Down Midshipman Ave. crossing Fortune Drive, we complete our ride at Garden of the Groves, created and named for the founder of Freeport. It's a tropical paradise of native floral plants and birds among waterfalls, shops andcafe.

Our tour concludes with a swim and a drive through the real Freeport, where people live their lives. Children in uniforms walk home, parents shop and work in this town the size of Galveston. Leroy shares his family's story. Heading back to the ship Leroy quizzes us on his lectures. We pass and he is pleased.

The tale of two tour guides: Denison, a 70-year-old white man comfortable in himself and in his small island, Key West, took us on a leisurely ride. Satisfied with what he has accomplished and who he has become.

A young man, Leroy, is solidly planted in his family and his young British Commonwealth country. He has aspirations which may go unfulfilled. Yet, he makes the most of his fate, smiling every day, welcoming tourists along a fast paced 12-mile bike ride. A proud young man who is on his way.

For me, a brief day with each gentleman, a tale of two guides. Many differences with much to learn from each, their purpose, plus who they are as people in their native habitats. I look forward to returning to their islands for more miles.

Maybe someday I will be able to welcome them to our island and miles of sidewalk along the seawall.

Post Script: On the next cruise to Freeport I could not locate Leroy's excursion. Hope all is well for him.

Mark Scibinico—*Elissa's* Bosun

Ballooning clouds of sails held down by three miles of tar covered lines propel *Elissa* across the Gulf. Sailors 100 feet above the sea released more sails, increasing the speed to nine whispering knots.

Amazingly, 600 dead tons in the iron hull is driven only by the wind. Miles of line and the crew control where the ship heads. Standing in the midst of this activity was the bosun, a young bearded man wearing a cap, quietly giving directions and encouragement. The year is 1877?

Actually, it's 2016. The ship is *Elissa*, built in 1877 at the height of the development of iron. Iron, that is still very hard, as my head-banging can attest.

Elissa, a complex machine, operates with only nature generating power as we glide along. The only actively sailed iron barque in the U.S., right here in Galveston. As interesting as the *Elissa* and its history may be, the bosun and port captain, Mark Scibinico, is equally interesting. The currents brought Mark to Galveston in 2012 when he oversaw the keel to truck (the top of the mast) overhaul of *Elissa*.

Dry-docked, hull panels were welded, steel to the 1877 still strong iron. The deck was replaced along with miles of new lines and sails. Mark's knowledge of traditional sailing ships was key to the historically correct restoration.

Born in Maryland close to the Chesapeake Bay, the sea was in Mark's blood from childhood. To learn historical square-rigged sailing meant going to sea for Mark. For years, he lived out of a sea bag, working his way up from cook to an able body sailor to bosun. He now holds a 200-ton captain's license. Mark has sailed to South America, all five Great Lakes and on the *Pride of Baltimore*. Once he delivered a sailboat from California to Florida. He participated in the New York City tall ship parade and mock naval battles.

A bosun, like a chief in the Navy or sergeant in the Army, is the link between officers and crew. At the Galveston Texas Seaport Museum, Mark's role is to work with over 75 volunteers. Volunteers contribute 30,000 hours of hard labor each year maintaining *Elissa*. Mark enjoys training groups of 70 new volunteers each summer.

"Our volunteers come for the program and stay for the friendship." Mark said, adding, "Sailing teaches you how to work with other people and with nature. Ship, shipmates and self, in that order."

Always outdoors, he rides his single speed bike to work. Not only does he juggle tasks at work, he is a real juggler, with bowling pins. Throughout his life experiences he has learned a multitude of skills, none of which include a computer—how refreshing. For more: www.galvestonhistory.org

Elissa heads out to sea with Bosun Mark

Lady, Smokey, Retirement and Wharf Walks

Dogs thrive on routine. With retirement, my routine certainly changed. No more rising at 4:30 a.m. Leaving an hour later, after a shower, cereal, morning joe and traffic reports. By the time the TV came on, the dogs, Lady and Smokey, would slowly wander out and plop down in their living room beds. With no big adieu, I would drop a treat in front of them as I hurried out the door.

Coming home was as frantic as the mornings were subdued. Smokey, wagged her whole long dachshund/lab body yelping and trying so hard not to jump up on me. She wiggled, sat, wiggled again, waiting for petting, acknowledgement, and praise. 14-year-old Lady would stretch and slow walk over to the door for a pat on the head. Soon we were out the door for a walk on the wharf or a roam in the dog park.

Now retirement days begin about 7:00 a.m., and after cereal and wishing there was less of Joe and more of his co-hosts, we are off for a walk. To the wharf if a ship is in, or the seawall for a late sunrise. During the day, trips to dog-friendly businesses and a late afternoon dog park visit with old friends. Maybe a late-night trip to Rita's Italian Ice on the seawall.

This new life style was quickly adopted as routine by the dogs, much better than their "master" (boy, that is a type of oxymoron!). My blood pressure is down, maybe due to weight loss, less stress, or my workouts each day. Truth is probably hanging out with the dogs and learning from their life style.

Trying to figure out what makes dogs tick (tick is probably not the best term to use around a dog) is the subject of many books and TV shows. After reading several books on dogs including, the *New York Times Big Book of Dogs* I learned a few things. Dogs sleep 70 percent of the time and Cesar the Dog Whisperer is the Baryshnikov of dog trainers.

So now with my shoulders back and with a firm voice we take real walks, not hunting and sniffing outings, as before. Oh, and now treats are employed for good behavior. They do have some influence.

Much of what I have learned about retirement is from Smokey, Lady and Pier 21. Enjoy what you are doing, meet new people and embrace simple routines. And get plenty of sleep.

A Unique Galveston Morning

Turning left onto Seawall Blvd. this late spring, almost light morning, I see the soft backlit cloud bank in the distance. The Ferris wheel and twisted roller coaster of Pleasure Pier materializes. Then ships. Fuchsia forms the bottom layer across the horizon laid on the blue water, while white wavelets lick the wide beach. Tractors with huge rakes smooth the sand.

Jimmy Buffet is singing, "Mother, Mother Ocean, you have seen it all. In your belly you can hold a treasure few have ever seen."

Another morning in Galveston. Finishing my iced coffee, sans ice—hey, it is only 77 this morning with a light breeze—still cool, I get the dogs out of the back. Parked for free this early in front of the beautifully landscaped San Luis, we have the same view as those paying so much more.

Blonde light stretches, then orange. A golden globe floats from the spectrum of color, the sun, a balloon, shines a beam of light across the aquatic scene. And they say I am color blind. With my clam phone I snap a shot so others can see.

Drawn to the dawn, we trek east, 15-year-old mostly border collie Lady has a bounce in her stride, Smokey, a lower to the ground dashador motors along. The iconic 1900 Great Storm sculpture, Poseidon, taking mother and child to the depths, by David W. Moore, reminds us that this view comes with a cost some Septembers.

After a respectful moment, we stroll on to Crockett Park, full of palm trees and sails. A peaceful oasis thanks to Frito Lay and Mayor Joe.

Still asleep on a bench is a gentleman straight out of casting from Pirates of the Caribbean. Bushy sideburns, a ponytail of grey, his bike efficiently loaded with baskets and a bag tied to the end—all of his possessions.

Regrettably, we turn our back to the view and head back. Seawall Blvd. has turned into the Indy 500 Speedway as insurance and medical employees from off the island race to work on the East End.

The sun is higher, the city alive, another day in an affordable paradise. Even for people living on the street. This morning, 6 a.m., a group of about ten folks without homes gathered as usual near the Golden Arches, sipping their coffee. In the dark they helped a friend stand up. A sight most do not see, yet a very real part of Galveston.

Just yesterday Gary Bell commented, "Galveston is such a unique place." He should know, a retired submarine captain, he has seen the world, even if he was under the sea for over two years.

Leaving the Park Board—it's Island Time—we were walking down 23rd Street toward the wharves, past Coffee Roaster's, Tammy at the insurance office, Bill Cherry's old Star Drugstore, yelling "Hi" to Cruz and a brief conversation about the day with a stranger who became an instant friend.

Yes, this is unique Galveston. Another day to cherish.

Chapter 5 – Cruising

Sitting on the Dock of the Port

Sitting on the dock of the bay, watching the ship cruise away without me, again. No other travel is the same as sailing out of port on a ship. Leaving in slow motion, time to take in the experience. Someday soon I will cruise out on that ship.

Driving from our house on 48th Street to 23rd to the cruise pier is easy, most of the time. One Easter departure, the cab dispatcher seemed unable to honor our reservations for noon. One o'clock came and went. Not wanting to miss our ship, I ran across the street to plead with our super neighbor, Pat Bartlett, for a ride to the port. I found her in the middle of dinner with friends.

Did I mention she is a super neighbor? She agreed and zipped down 51st Street to the ship. Since then another cab company has been our reliable, on time replacement.

I always wanted to ride my bike to the cruise ship, suitcase in the doggy trailer. The problem is where to park my bike. It might cost as much as a car.

Arriving at the cruise terminal is an experience. People pour out of cars, cabs and buses, all carrying far too much. Excitement is in the air and the bell caps, in colorful Hawaiian shirts, pile suitcases high on their carts, promising that every item will be delivered to your stateroom on board. Stuffing tips in their pockets they whisk your bags away.

You grab your carry-on bag, with your medicine, one change of clothes, and all of your documents. Entering the terminal building you present your papers, for the first of many times, to a part-time, often retired, cruise line representative.

Then you get in line for an easy screening, walking through

the metal detector. Up the escalator to another snaking line where you wait until you are called to one of numerous stations at the counter.

At the counter, you receive your cruise card and are directed to another line where you pause for a photo op. Next, is the long gangway to the ship. Presenting your card to the ship's security guard, your photo is checked and you wander into an expansive atrium to the sound of party music.

Now begins your Alice in Wonderland experience, trying to find your cabin. Off for lunch on the top deck and you begin to relax realizing this trip is really happening.

After checking your cabin a few more times to see if your bags have arrived, the muster station (abandon ship) drill begins. Time to count the lifeboats, times 45, divided into 2,500 people. Okay, there are enough.

Back on the Lido deck, topside, you watch the ship slowly move from the wharf and begin our trip. After 65 years of flying, I don't even notice takeoffs. On a ship, I notice. You roam around a 1,000- foot stage to find the best view. And you wave and yell good-bye to those on the wharves.

Hey, I can see my house from up here. The best view is seeing the *Elissa* slip past the stern as we head out. Who cares where we are going? I don't. My ship has left, this time with me.

Cruising puts a smile on my face, too

Terminal Observations and Hawaiian Shirts

Peacefully sitting in the largest single berth cruise-ship terminal in the world watching disembarkation provides one a new perspective on life. I am waiting while Port of Galveston Police Officer Mike Washington checks on a possible arrest (not mine). I am doing a ride-along this morning. Hawaiian shirts, cut-off jeans and t-shirts flip-flop by at a hurried shuffle, dragging wheeled mini-homes.

Red-shirted staff ask arriving passengers if they have any cigarettes or liquor. Are the Red-shirts short of money? No, they just want to be sure the taxpayers of Texas get our fair share of tariff taxes.

Carefully spaced customs agents process passengers. A composed mom holding a toddler's hand is smiling. Why? She is getting off the lap of luxury, where the beds are made, meals prepared, and babysitters available. Must be getting home is still better.

Seasoned cruisers are easy to spot, backpacks, small suitcases, running shoes and no extra shopping bags. Wearing recently purchased t-shirts, you know they just came back from Belize, Roatan and Mexico. Streamlined, they quickly pass others on their way to the airport buses.

Porters in even more Hawaiian shirts (I love them too, Cruz) tug large four-wheel racks, stacked high with cases, bags hanging from hooks. They steer through the crowd followed by a gaggle of folks, straining to stay in contact with their belongings.

Two cruise ships are in port this morning, almost 8,000 people off and another 8,000 on with tons of luggage. Meanwhile semi- trucks bumper to bumper pull up to loading docks. Forklifts dart in and out like humming birds to a flower rushing meat, veggies, eggs, soda, and of course liquor aboard. Other lifts dash in the other doorway with pallets of, you guessed it, suitcases.

Officer Washington returns and we walk across the street in front of the terminal. The back of a large SUV is packed solid with suitcases. Dad stands holding yet another bag, staring at the suitcase wall while three other bags lie at his feet.

Good luck, sir.

Cars dart in and out, no eyes looking forward, that is toward us. Several officers have been hit, none seriously—a bulletproof vest is evidently not enough protection for this traffic. As we arrived, a SUV changed to our lane, head-on, and then cut off a bus. Officer Washington just shook his head and said the ship was not going to leave for several hours, wondering what their rush is. I wanted to go arrest the driver, but at that rate, the jail would be full of eager tourists.

Okay, before you hear it from my relatives, I used to be one. Now we arrive later to an almost empty terminal. Taking a cruise is so much fun that behavioral lapses may be excused. Port Police officers calmly shake their heads at such actions knowing there are far worse crimes. A critical observation at the terminal, otherwise we wouldn't need Port Police.

Nicole's Triumph *By Alvin and Nicole Sallee*

Our granddaughter Nicole sits comfortably on the large ocean view window ledge aboard the cruise ship *Triumph*. We just sailed past Fort Point, down the channel out into the sunset. Close by, the pilot boat, *Texas,* bucked as we crossed the Sabine-Freeport current. Slowing, the pilot hopped off as the lights of Galveston glowed in the distance.

Picking up my book *Torpedoes in the Gulf*, recommended by Capt. Vandy, I realize it may be not the most reassuring book to read while transiting to Mexico's Yucatan over 12,000-foot-deep waters.

Today we celebrated Memorial Day, 73 years after U-boats, Gray Wolves, entered the Gulf waiting in these same waters to sink merchant ships and tankers. Fifty-six were sunk in the Gulf during WWII, and fourteen damaged. Several were repaired in the Todd Yard in Galveston. The *Robert E. Lee* lies below, close to the U-166 submarine that sank her, both recently explored by the E/V *Nautilus*.

Next day brings sunshine and navy blue waters as we explored the Mayan world on the Yucatan and swam with dolphins. Tied beside *Magic* (the ship and the emotion), a skyscraper canyon is formed. It's just like New York City right here in Cozumel, including East Coast-type crowds pushed through the shopping gauntlet.

The lines dropped away as the huge ship eased from the wharf. Half a mile out, the Pilot boat, *Manatee*, approached allowing the t-shirted pilot to step from the *Triumph*, waving goodbye, his act complete.

Nicole dropped into her window ledge sofa/bed and asked me how much money I had left on my credit card. Good question, I was just wondering that myself. Why? She is looking over the gift shop flyers from Cozumel. Jewelry questions follow, like, "How much is $1,999?" I explain it's a sales pitch, for $2,000. After further discussion, I am glad she chose the $15 shark tooth necklace over topaz.

That evening passing the Excursion Desk, I asked Elvis (real name) what trips we could experience the next day—a sea day? He calmly answered my smart aleck question: The behind the scenes tour and he had two tickets left. Can an 8-year-old go? "Yes," he answered. Now I guess I have to buy them.

The succeeding day we hiked all over the ship, behind the glitter. We walked on the steel deck plates that lined I-95, the corridor which runs the length of the ship. We passed through the crew's lounge, offices, laundry, freezers, warehouses for suitcases, control room, all the way to the galley at the stern.

On the bridge, we were careful not to touch any knobs during our visit and picture with the captain. Exit stage right down to the theater. In a small dressing room—I've seen larger closets in *Coast Monthly* magazine—Greg, the lead dancer, explained how the cast makes fifteen costume changes during each show.

Morning brought buoys and downtown. The streets of Galveston glided by as we returned to doing our wash and making our own beds. This first cruise met Nicole's moral of the story—always have fun!

Dreams the Same as Ours

Beat after three hours boarding the ship in Bayport or is it Pasadena? Or Houston? Flopping down in my *Princess* bed, sans pea, I begin scanning the tours for Progresso. Having visited the Yucatan for thirty years I find nothing new.

Good thing we made other plans. Canadian friends that we met on a cruise winter in Progresso, but now they are visiting India. They suggested a cruise ship volunteer tour, Chix Food Bank.

It's run by Sharon, a retired Canadian nurse, who arrived sixteen years ago. Working with many volunteers including the "Beach Gals" (Americans and Canadians), they assist kids to seniors, food to healthcare. For a decade, she has arranged volunteer tours. It is almost free.

Website: http://foodbankchicxulub.com/

Following instructions to meet a couple from the ship at cab number 33, we all piled in and were off to Chicxulub, about ten miles east. The young thirty-something couple was from Katy via Illinois where they both grew up.

Our driver, Gustavo, of Mayan descent, volunteers with the charity partly to learn English. He really doesn't seem to need much practice.

Driving through the small-town streets with high walls sheltering homes, he is proud of his hometown of 6,000. Like in Galveston, a few stray dogs wander along the streets in the fresh humid morning air.

Arriving at the school, the young Katy woman pulled me aside. She is shocked by such "poverty" and trash. I am surprised; this is a very nice middle class Mexican neighborhood; many of the condos are owned by expats.

"This is my first time outside of the U.S.," she responds. "Oh," I answer, thinking this ignorance is what shapes our foreign policy. The Katy couple decide to hire the cab for a more conventional tourist tour of Mayan sites.

Entering the school, we are greeted by bright-eyed grade school children in clean ironed uniforms. Soon it becomes obvious the kids know much more about the USA than we of

Mexico. Teachers are serious about learning and it shows. School assignments reveal excellent math skills.

During recess, I spy some 10-year-old boys using a basketball for soccer (futbol) on the court. After having them throw it around a while, I dunk. Okay, the rim is 8 feet, but still it's a dunk and I'm 65. They laughed. As I walked away, they go back to kicking the basketball around.

With Kay and Sharon, our walking tour through Chicxulub began by visiting the library, markets, mothers, workers and new pier. People are so friendly and gracious, no entitlement here. They try English—clearly, we are off the tourist trail—me, Spanish. Somehow, we communicate.

Kay drove us to Progresso, the "big city". Thousands of tourists pour off cruise ships, some trashing the beaches, coarse and staggering back to the ships drunk. A few ugly Americans create a terrible impression of all of us. Wonder if that is true for Muslims too? It is.

Unfamiliarity of other cultures fuels fears fanned by politicians resulting in potentially ugly policies. If more of us travel internationally, maybe we'll be thankful for more than football and cyber Mondays. We might understand that a little trash blowing in the street doesn't mean people have dreams dissimilar from ours.

Not-So-Boring Days at Sea

"So, are you going to write about me?" she asked. Staring out at the indigo deep blue sea, hands gripping the mahogany rail in a captain-like stance, I drift back to reality, if there is such a thing on a ship in the Caribbean. I look down to see Pat. Twinkling eyes behind large glasses. Her smile is framed by probably well-earned silver hair. Her husband Ed stands next to her, appearing professorial.

"Sure," I answered, wondering how they knew I write a newspaper column. Had the Galveston County Daily News expanded to Williamson County, where they live? Maybe, after all, I hear from readers from all over.

Pat explained she is a member of a writing club and allows

she might like to read some interesting wharf stories. Each evening we sit at the same dinner table with eight other people, yet I don't remember mentioning the column.

We stood at this same rail a week ago while leaving St. Maarten. They pointed out the *Stars and Stripes* sailed by Dennis Connors when he won the America's Cup. The couple excitedly recounted their adventure that afternoon blazing across the bay aboard the twelve-metre boat. These 70-something-year-olds were like kids recounting a visit to the Pleasure Pier.

Now I remembered, I mentioned I had written a column about my sail boat race in Cozumel, promising I would email them a copy. Boy does Pat have a memory.

Another morning we had a leisurely sea day breakfast getting to know each other. This is a second marriage of twenty-five years for both of them. They met at a church singles event. Ed had a German Shepherd, she three cats and four kids. While maybe it wasn't love at first sight, clearly something clicked, as they appear to be a very happy seasoned couple.

Ed, an MIT graduate, worked for defense contractors on smart bombs. They followed his job from Lewisville to Tucson and finally to Georgetown—Texas not D.C. As a nurse, Pat could find a job anywhere. In her last position, she traveled all over evaluating hospitals.

Ed wrote a book on World War II, *The Other Doolittle Raid*, a gripping day-by-day portrayal of the war. He sent me a thumb drive and I read a few pages each day. We are coming up to 75 years after Pearl Harbor this year. A very timely read.

You certainly meet interesting people on a three-week cruise, even a dog or two. Sarge is a therapy dog, actually Helping Dog of the Year for 2015.He and his master are on for the full cruise. Boy, could my dogs take lessons from Sarge.

Sea days on the itinerary look boring, yet in reality they can be as informative as a cultural tour on an island.

Time to visit with this guy I met bouncing in a small boat going over to St. John's. Kelly is a history buff. Come to find out we both had Prof. Snodgrass at Phillips University in the late 1960's. We spend hours laughing and reminiscing. Hey, where did the day go?

Traveling the World: Breakfast at Sea

What a contrast. Breakfast at home is oatmeal in the microwave and instant coffee with almond cream. Plop down on my chair in front of Morning Joe.

Breakfast on a ship is so different. First, I am faced with a fifty-mile-long buffet. Second, which table to sit at. Sit with a stranger with a view or a viewless table for two, by myself? Which exotic juice? Coffee, decaf or full strength? It's 4:30 a.m. on Galveston time, so I am not at full speed.

My answers: Skip the buffet line and go for oatmeal with fruit. Guava juice watered down, decaf with fat free milk. Two-person table with across-the-room view of the azul Caribbean.

We are 17 degrees north. I am contemplating that the water is 21,000 feet deep here as we sail over the Cayman Trench.

"Hey, Alvin!" Emerging from my ocean analysis, I see new friends in the scenic section next to the Texas-size windows. Steve and Marilyn know Laura and Robert, friends I made on a cruise to Key West last year. Small world. Laura and Marilyn became friends while working on a project in the Ukraine years ago and vacationed in Columbia, or something like that.

Marilyn worked as a nurse in several countries before recently retiring. Having started new meds, I am low energy right now. Some nurses don't want to hear about people's ills. Yet, Marilyn listens and agrees with my amateur assessment.

We launch into solving healthcare in the U.S. and around the world. Both she and Steve have had medical experiences in Germany and England—from both sides of the scalpel. After an hour of facts, research and a heavy dose of common sense, we conclude healthcare is a right. It must be paid for somehow. An additional hour explores options—do away with insurance companies, get rid of paper, go online, more family and nurse practitioners? We decide we need to keep profits from driving healthcare.

Time to discuss travels. Worst traffic? Houston and Chihuahua. Most beautiful women and roses? Colombia. Worst roads? Where there is rain and no asphalt.

"Would you like some more coffee?" Dora from Hungary asks. "Oh, hi," I reply. Dora waits on me at dinner too, knowing to mix the strong iced tea with water in my glass.

We all begin discussing Buda, of Budapest fame, Dora's hometown. Marcus of Romania, the busboy, joins the conversation.

He adds that the U.S. faces the future, while Europe looks to the past. (This was before Trump was elected.)

We come back to discussing Galveston. The two young staff rate various ports by Wi-Fi strength. Starbucks is okay; Seafarers Center is a sanctuary. As a small port, Galveston doesn't have much to do for these 20-year-olds with only five hours off. Actually, three for Marcus—he sleeps two hours before leaving the ship.

It's almost noon when we finish solving the world's problems. We have traveled through Europe, South America and the U.S. at the breakfast table. Another "freebie" of cruising I don't get at home watching TV. Now what's for lunch and where will I sit?

Magic Time with Special Needs

What began as a joke birthday present, ended up as a cruise for my mother. A great deal and huge cabin for persons with limited mobility clinch it.

Mother is a high IQ, MBA, star volunteer, sports fan and former world traveler. At ninety-two, she uses a walker and has limited sight. With courage, daily exercise, and the ADA, she gets around amazingly, just maybe slower than the turtles she loves.

The ship's agent spent an hour addressing her questions, even knowing there are eleven steps to the tender in Belize. Still it takes several days for us to locate the ship's three fully-handicapped accessible restrooms.

Mother agrees to use a wheelchair at the airport. Bringing

her "Cadillac" walker which converts to a wheelchair, albeit with smaller wheels. Pulling up to the wharf, a polite port police officer, when informed we have a passenger in a wheelchair, points us toward the entrance of Terminal One. Gliding the car between the cones to the curb is slick—an "A+" for accessibility (read last paragraph). We quickly unloaded.

Next challenge: the wharf maze to the supersized cabin. It's 12:30 p.m. Mother wants lunch on board and to use her "wheelchair". Did I mention the wheels are small? Not good for door jams. A bit of body English (mine, not hers), we make it inside the terminal. Quickly funneled to TSA, the agents make it easy and yet thorough. Up to a line for cabin cards. Smile, snap and off we went.

"Because it is there" may be a reason to climb Mt. Everest, but not the ramp to the ship. A no-go for small wheels, after hearing "I don't know" from several staff part-timers. Walkie-talkie toting Debbie ordered real wheelchairs. A wounded Veteran joined us. Soon a fleet of chair "pushers" arrived whisking us up to the cruise ship *Magic*'s lobby. Back on the walker, we waited for an elevator, like everyone else.

The 11th deck cabin was right over the bow. The assigned dining room almost 1,000 feet to the rear, seven decks down. After a meeting with the Maître d' our dining site is moved about 500 feet forward. When boarding elevators, my basketball rebound stance comes in handy until folks realize there is enough food aboard. Then politeness emerges. People hold doors offering, "Take your time."

Mother loves being on ships, so she only got off briefly in Cozumel. No jumping from the speedboat in Belize required. Returning to the Galveston wharf, the staff used a real wheelchair to disembark, just after Platinum.

A short wait in line two and we were waved through to the curb. With the walker, we didn't have far to go to the cone zone. Then, boom. A non-port-officer lets me know in no uncertain terms that there is no driving into the cone zone. Mother says, "If you can't say anything good ..."

Okay then, no more comments regarding the incident. Just know there's no parking in the cone zone. We still had a Magic time.

Musical Travel, Galveston to Buenos Aires

Folks driving on the Island label themselves by the route they travel. Captain Vandy is a Seawall guy, with Chief Mac Broadway bound. BOI's (Born on the Islanders) are P and O'ers, straight through. A few are Q'ers, often over the speed limit. Make me a Harborsider all the way, 51st to Holiday. Have to see what is going on at the wharves.

Drivers who are not talking or texting—yes, there are a few of us, very few, I am afraid, listen to the radio. For me it is 89.5 to 25th Street, then 90.1. They are the same station, KFPT. Roark, Texas DJ of the year, plays a kaleidoscope of music, mellow Monday, through wild Friday. It is commercial free, but it is not free, so if you listen, pledge and pay your fair share.

The three-masted *Elissa* at the Seaport Museum wharf is home to musical sea shanties this month.

Then there is the wonderful Galveston Symphony Orchestra, playing concerts in The Grand 1894 Opera House, taking patrons on musical rides throughout the year. Four concerts still remain.

The recent performance was quite a trip. Billed as the Halloween Concert, it began with the Funeral March of a Marionette. Boo! A Tango for Cello and Strings brought us to Buenos Aires through the fingers of guest soloist Brinton Smith.

Side note, Mr. Smith's cello performances can be heard on CBS Sunday Morning, American Public Media's Performance Today, and Symphony cast. His recordings include a solo with the New Zealand Symphony. Plus, he has played with Yo-Yo Ma. With a Doctorate of Musical Arts, Professor Smith is on the Rice University Faculty.

Admitted to Arizona State University at age 10, Mr. Smith became a Teaching Assistant by nineteen with an M.A. in math. I attended ASU as well. Let's just say I graduated with a master's.

As a third grader, I also wanted to play the cello. We had a piano. After a year of paying for piano lessons, Mother allowed me to play the basketball. Wise.

Now back to the music. A duet stretched strings between a million-dollar violin and a hugely eloquent, impassioned cellist. Called the "impossible duet", it was possible. I heard it from the Grand Tier.

Off to Norway and the story of the troll told through musical version of a boy's travels. He always avoided obstacles till meeting the devil. A new score was written by Harald Saeverud, the grandfather of our tour guide, and Tround Saeverud, the GSO Conductor.

Off to our final destination, Disneyland. Well actually, The Sorcerer's Apprentice by Dukas. Better known from Walt Disney's animated film, Fantasia, starring Mickey Mouse. The kettledrums and bassoons are the stars. In a Victor Borge-like manner, Conductor Saeverud points out that Disney stayed very close to each measure. And could those brooms dance.

For a guy who is not allowed to whistle while others are in the car and whose best instrument is the stereo, I really enjoyed this trip. To join in on the next adventure visit: www.galvestonsymphony.com.

Arriving in Port

Pitch dark, yet I am wide-awake. Rolling over I hit the clock's light. It's 5:30 a.m. I turn on the TV channel with the bow camera view. Against an almost black screen two bright lights mark the jetties. Nuts, I need to get up to see us arrive in port.

A few moments later, aft on deck 11, looking down I see a small tanker quietly pass us. This channel is narrow. In our wake, in the false forty shades of grey dawn, the pilot boat lazily follows, moving to and fro.

Okay, once again I'm glad I got up early, but now I'm hungry. With a bowl of oatmeal (I think it is) and cup of coffee, I'm soon back on the stern. We glide by the parking lot at Fort Point where with the dogs I often watch ships leaving in the afternoon.

The scene from a hundred feet up is stunning. The sunrise on the horizon becomes a Rachel Wiley-Janota painting—yellows, greens and pale pink blending into the sea.

A line of ships head up the channel to Houston past the *Selma*, a concrete ship beached in the 1920's, now buffeted by waves of days gone past. The ferry whips around Seawolf Park, a white mustache on its bow.

Another passenger joins me on the stern. I mention that soon we will be at the front, as the ship will rotate and back up the channel to dock. He says no, it will turn at the pier, not before. I mention the cruise ship *Triumph* does that but this ship, the *Breeze*, is larger and backs up. He strongly disagrees.

Not interested in getting into an argument at 6:00 a.m., I let it drop as the ship begins to turn. His misinformation reminds me of how little most of us know about the Port's operation.

Now the stern is headed first down the waterway. Standing on the Galveston Island side, I wonder, when a ship is backing up, does the port side become the starboard? At least now I know enough folks around the Port who can tell me. (It doesn't.)

We pass landmarks, the Galveston Naval Museum, USS *Stewart* and *Cavella*, the Yacht basin, with the yacht *GreY* (yes, that's correct) *Mist* nodding good morning. A bulk carrier, empty, rides high in the sky above. The Island is so tiny from up here, even UTMB is small. The RO/RO and banana ship docks slide by as the Mosquito Fleet masts gently sway in the whiting light.

The Ocean Star rig, then *Elissa's* three masts and we are at our wharf. More cargo ships still further down the channel.

Clearly there is much more to the Port of Galveston than cruise ships. This is a very busy place even early in the morning.

More wharf stories to explore. Who sails the shrimp boats? How is the traffic in the Port controlled? Who loads the ships? What is up with all of those railroad cars? Who casts off the lines? As Laura Elder writes, stay tuned.

Make Galveston a Port of Call

"No mother, we did not need to go to Houston. All the attractions were within two miles of our home on Galveston Island," I answered over the phone. Our kids and granddaughters had just visited us for a busy week.

The list was long. Their top three were: a swimming park, the harbor tours and a sporting goods store. Eating establishments were a hit too. Shrimp and catfish first tried by the girls with their noses in the air accompanied by a frown until the first flavors seeped into their tongues.

Driving around, from the historic east-end through UTMB, along the sea wall to the west-end, returning on Harborside. The cruise ships did salute. Up and down O and P Streets, with the style at the Garten Verein, an octagon Great Storm survivor in Kempner Park.

Off to the wonderful aquarium to meet Jimi Hendrix, the penguin. Next-door, a tall jungle in a huge pyramid. Later an indoor Disney like river adventure boat ride after more seafood on the seawall. Many walks and bike rides along the 33 miles of beach with swims in the warm waters.

Did I mention food? A five-star feast before a matinee at the 1894 Grand Opera House. Acoustics and architecture found in very few places. It is only a few blocks from the wharf, not to mention an ocean oil rig.

Throughout downtown we rode in a horse drawn white carriage viewing Clayton and Muller structures plus carved live oak trees. Distant and recent past intertwined. Electric golf carts, duck boats and soon trolley cars, all available to tour the past.

"Want to get on the water?" I asked. Kayaks in the marsh, sailing boats across Offatts Bayou, and in the port seeking dolphins by boat. Or twisted in all sorts of directions in an orange rocket boat.

Ferry boat rides on me.

We called on vessels of the dramatic past. Sitting on Pelican Island in Seawolf Park are the destroyer escort, USS *Stewart*, and submarine, USS *Cavalla*. Welcome aboard. Where else can you climb and crawl through craft in starring roles of WWII undersea warfare? Stand on their proud bows pointed out to the Gulf to see a parade of ships sail through five channels all at once.

Into the wild West? Galveston has the best, found in a restored 1800's children's home. Or see some films of pirates and hurricanes next to the tall ship *Elissa*. Walk through the door from Saengerfest Square to be face to face with pirates fighting hand-to-hand. All aboard a true train museum, papier-mâché 1930's folks await. Shopping? Oh, my. Hawaiian shirts, t-shirts too, athleisure wear to tea kettles, antiques to Mardi Gras masks, it's all here.

Art catch your fancy? Are you in luck. Galleries painted between history, restaurants through the Strand and surrounds. What friendly people. But, am I worn out. Wish I could climb into a cruise ship bed with glorious Galveston memories in my head. It's island time for a port of call.

Port of Call Consideration

A distinguished panel just discussed issues related to Galveston as a port of call. I was not invited to participate; perhaps because I was at sea? As a briefcase-toting traveler, I qualify as an expert consultant, having visited over thirty ports of call from Nawiliwili to Istanbul. Well, at least I should be in a focus group.

So, this is to let the powers that be know I am available to testify but only when not on a cruise ship, working on the USS *Stewart* or sailing at Sea Star Base.

Seriously, as a participant observer researcher of third world to US ports, I'm prepared to compare them to Galveston. Reader alert: Galveston does very well. Maybe not the best but I can't return to the Bosporus for a while.

Why Galveston? Galveston is accessible, has plenty of potential varied excursions, is historical and has the largest single ship terminal. Best of all the mystique of Galveston sells.

Ships can easily dock a block from the Strand. Plenty of room to organize tours in the shade of Terminal One.

We have excursions potential galore in the city and country. What about a quick trip to NASA, or sailing in the bays? Walk over to the Texas Seaport Museum and board an 1877 sailing ship? How about a tour through downtown reading the historic plaques, shopping (taxes), eating (taxes), and watching the fountains in Hendley Green? Trolley ride anyone?

Catch a Duck Boat tour with George, Segway to harbor tours or a morning living in World War II aboard USS *Cavalla* and *Stewart* in Seawolf Park?

Thrill rides at the Pleasure Pier and Schlitterbahn Waterpark or Pier 21? Museums? We have a bunch: the Bryan, Moody Gardens, Rosenberg and even carved trees—what a nice day.

Oh, I have dibs on rock-stacking at Crockett Park on the Seawall. I'll hire some civil engineering students, put up some tents and get a photographer to record everyone's creativity (jobs). Then maybe off to East Beach for sand castle building, a swim and a kayak trip with Artist Boat in the lagoon.

A ferry boat ride (it's on me) to Bolivar Peninsula for a walking tour of Fort Travis, after it gets fixed and then birdwatching?

Biking on the Seawall, stopping to view the bench artwork? By the way, Tampa claims their 4.5-mile sidewalk is the longest in the world. Sorry Tampa, you're about 6 miles short. Our list can go on, but I only have five hundred words.

We like to have fun, welcome newcomers and we can brag a bit too. We have plenty of folks who like to work—yes even retirees. The police forces know how to handle crowds in a friendly manner. We have tons of vans and we are great at organizing events. A restroom on each block, a little clean up and we are ready. I am available to provide more details. I work cheap. Just give me rhubarb pie.

PS: Later I was asked to consider joining the Port of Call committee, no mention of pie. We will see. Key Lime is good, too.

A Russian Sub in Galveston Bay?

Through many shades of slate grey, an image emerges appearing like a Russian Typhoon class submarine, sans conning tower. German subs were off the Galveston beaches during WWII, but now the shape is one of several large black geo-textile tubes creating an artificial breakwater which allows small islands of sea grasses to grow.

Good, the marsh mounds protect parts of the coast during a hurricane I selfishly contemplate while sitting in my kayak. Our guide, Cherie explains this is habitat for birds. Clearly it is birding season. I see more egrets, frigates and blue heron in a minute than I have in a month driving around. Mullets do back flips out of the water. Dolphins in training?

We are on a three-hour tour. The Skipper, Mary Ann (now you know my choice), the Professor (of course), the millionaires and Gilligan, for a three-hour tour—in kayaks. A very polite and interesting couple, hey, from Canada, is with us too. After touring all over the U.S., they found Galveston. Buying a condo on the beach. In a couple of years, retirement will bring them here permanently.

Hope they keep their health insurance! Mine is a lousy B&B. Not being a BOI or BIT (this is your crossword puzzle time), I wish we had the Canadian version of healthcare. No emails, please, look it up online.

Back to our expedition on the Coastal Heritage Preserve. Artist Boat has saved 360 acres of bay lands and a Texas General Land Office grant reduces the tour costs to only $10 a person. Everything is included. You can register at www.artistboat.org.

This is nature: beautiful, tranquil, and restful. A paddle quietly gurgles and the birds discuss politics or where to go next. There is a pecking order here (no pun intended). The 747-wingspan blue heron are queens of the marsh.

Thanks to the BodySpace's Courtney's Pilates torture sessions (only kidding), my powerhouse (gut) easily propels me through the small waterways. On the way back, which was much, much further than I thought, I make good progress, almost sprinting. Cherie is barely paddling and yet going as fast. Clue: not only is she a marine biology graduate, she was the lead position on the Texas A&M at Galveston's crew. The fancy skinny rowboats.

We discuss the Artist Boat program for 6th graders through high school students. Out here she teaches STEM, with PE and art—a total curriculum, all in kayaks. Wow! Typing on her small TV-size phone, even out here, Cherie informs us, "According to radar, we'll barely make it to shore before the storm hits."

As the kayaks move apart (okay, I fall behind), I ponder, how hundreds of years ago the Karankawa, speaking in Aula, survived storms? How did they live? Sharing this experience, traveling in the same mode, it is easy to reflect in this special place.

Thank you, Artist Boat, for the voyage through time and for Cherie's phone. We just beat the rain.

Moore Island? Keep Paddling

Too late—I bet the weekend trip is full. Going online (www.artistboat.org), we are surprised that there are 16 slots available. OK, let's sign up. We are off on a four-hour tour of the Conservation Preserve via kayaks with Artist Boat.

On this pleasant sunny morning, everyone lathers up in sunscreen topped off in bug spray. Bags are checked for water tightness and stored away in plastic art boxes on the stern of each kayak.

Paddles are laid out. We get to choose our color and number and clip each together, so one blade is not feathered. Hey, this is a birding trip.

While waiting on a few late folks we hear the word "Albuquerque" our ears perk up. Yes, these people really are from our hometown. And they know our friends at New Mexico State University and even at UTEP. We are one of three New Mexico families rowing today.

Alex, our guide, gives us a thorough safety orientation and we zip up our vests—I fit this time. Soon ten double orange ocean kayaks are pulled out into the brown warm water. To get in first we sit on our bottoms and then swing our legs in—with a 36" inseam, easier said than done in my case.

Teamed with my 8-year-old granddaughter, Nicole, there is no doubt where I sit. Heaviest in the stern, my place. Her job is to paddle providing power and I steer, that is what I hear Alex say. Nicole's translation: captain is in the front and my job is to paddle when commanded, which turns out to be always. Reaching the grass islands, we sight herons, egrets, the always-graceful pelicans—except for their belly flops. A stingray is just below the surface.

Scene from Moore Island aboard artist boat

Beaching on Moore Island we stretch our legs while munching on peanut butter sandwiches. Walking over to Alex's boat, we see she is eating juicy watermelon. That looks so good. She replies, "It's not as cold as I would like." "Want to trade for a warm sandwich?" No go.

Back on the calm waters we head to the other side for watercolor painting. Nicole gets right to work. I pass, my first Artist Boat painting took the prize for fully uniform grey, even though I used every color.

Soon a couple of ladies bump into us, literally. We have a nice chat, as Nicole begins painting the next canvas. Total and full concentration, no indication of engagement in our conversation. Less than a half hour later she produces two masterpieces, now "framed" on our refrigerator.

Heading back now I realize, as blisters begin to form, why my bike gloves were left on my kayak shoes. Nicole picks up the pace. Experienced from my last "race", we cut the tangent going from last to beating her mom and dad to shore. As Artist Boat founder Karla Klay quotes an African proverb: "To go fast, go alone; to go far, go together"—success all around.

Chapter 6 - Panama Canal

Panama Canal at 100

Five a.m.—First, the false dawn over the Pacific, then the lights of Panama City. In the calm warm November morning, I lean on the rail waiting. Waiting for the sun to come up over the Pacific. Waiting to experience the Panama Canal on the Norwegian Cruise Line's *Jewel.* We have traveled from Los Angeles, stopping in several ports, heading for Houston.

The events that led me to this place began in 1951. My father was called to active duty serving as the executive officer on a destroyer patrolling the Caribbean, just north of the Panama Canal. As a result, my Mother and I moved to the D.C. Naval Yard, Dad's homeport.

Last summer during a trip to Turkey I learned that in 1453 the Turks retook Istanbul along with pirates to the south which disrupted trade between Europe and Asia. So, Columbus sailed west looking for another route to India. On his fourth attempt, in 1503, he found Panama, just two miles from the modern canal, and only 50 land miles from the Pacific.

We take on the pilots and 21 linemen and queue up for our ship's turn through the Canal. The first buoy marks the channel, gliding past as the waking city slowly moves astern. Approaching the narrower channel at 7:30 a.m., I am pressed up against the rail as other passengers strain to see. Little do they care that we would have a full ten hours to drink in everything. Most of as have waited a lifetime to see this wonder.

How in the 1530's did explorers ever consider a canal over these mountains and through this jungle, disease, and rainfall? And how did the French and then the Americans apply the engineering, geological, political and epidemiological skills (and money) to cut through mountains, create the largest manmade lake and thus the canal to unite the world?

Twenty-five thousand workers, mostly from Caribbean countries, paid with their lives. Disease and dynamite took most lives.

The Bridge of the Americas soars above us as buses rush over honking with people waving madly from the windows. Clearly, they do not see Pan Max cruise ships every morning. Tugboats come to our side, but don't touch. The *Jewel* will make the trip under her own power. The tugs are for insurance. Just ahead of us, a bulk carrier squeezes into the port (left) lock. The six stories tall lock doors close behind its stern, causing the ship to appear to levitate. Unseen to us, millions of gallons of water rushes in raising the ship 45 feet.

We enter the starboard lock, and eight powerful mule engines on each side tie on, not to move us, but to maintain the narrow two-foot space between the ship and the lock wall. In a later lock, I easily touched the wall—it was less than two feet. What a balancing act. The *Jewel* is 965 feet long. The locks are 1,000 feet long. Thus the "Max" in our title.

In one set of locks we are beside a bulk carrier—only feet separate the ships. Their crew lounges on the deck with little to do. I strike up a conversation with them in my limited Spanish and they smile and wave like mad as I take their photo. I am surprised at their enthusiasm until I notice one of the cute young woman trainers from our ship standing next to me.

After two locks, we cross the small Miraflores Lake and after one more lock we are eighty-five feet higher than sea level, ready to enter the nine-mile Culebra Cut. When you see old movies of the dirt flying, chances are the long ditch, which is the Cut, is on the screen under construction.

The French began the canal in 1881 following the route of the railroad, opened in 1855. By the way, thanks to the White family, the Galveston Railroad Museum has a wonderful display on the Panama Canal Railroad and a great hand-drawn 3-D aerial map. After trying to cut a sea-level canal, the French were forced to abandon construction. They were a few years too early, before health measures, a free Panama and larger equipment. The U.S. took over the canal building in 1904. A U.S. battleship helped "maintain the peace" during Panama's bloodless revolution from Colombia.

We enter the Culebra Cut, second in a one-way convoy of seven ships. With only a 300-ft. wide bottom, the Cut is too narrow to pass other wide ships. Mountain peaks on either side signify the Continental Divide. The numbers regarding the Cut are difficult to comprehend. Enough material was excavated to build 63 Egyptian pyramids. One hundred million yards removed by 6,000 workers every day with hundreds of railcars.

Today the Canal is adding another "lane". Port side is almost finished, new third set of canal locks, ten stories high. Construction has begun on the two-mile-long dam, which will feed new Max ships into the cut.

Close-up of original Canal Gate—still in operation

Current Pan Max container ships can hold 4,500 containers; the new canal will allow new Max ships with 12,000 containers, almost three times larger. Not much longer, just wider, like I am getting on this cruise.

The pilot uses large "billboard" signs on the distant shore to guide the ship through the channel. Lining the bow up with these signs helps keep the ship on course, while making numerous curving turns. Emerging from the cut, I expect to see a wide expanse of water. Gatun Lake spreads like hundreds of fingers for miles toward the mountains. The ship looks like it was placed in a small West Texas lake by the giant hand of a child. The land barely moves back and we begin to narrowly pass by many small islands.

Glancing up, I'm shocked to see superstructures of other ships slide by in the other direction, appearing within arm's reach. Everyone waves.

Panama City at dawn—another day

It was decided to dam the Chagres River and create the lake to operate the locks and generate electricity. The canal now crosses over the old Chagres River bed under the lake over twenty times.

The river drains a large protected rain forest into the lake. With a rainy season of nine months that is a lot of water until you consider it takes 52 million gallons of water per ship to cross through the locks.

During the drought in the late 1960's, USS *Sturgis* operated a nuclear power plant in the canal, thus freeing up enough water for an additional 13 ships per day to pass through the canal.

The Gatun earthen dam is overgrown and runs for about a mile and a half alongside us, invisible until you see the small spillway. The dam is almost half a mile wide at the base. The spillway will be raised about one foot to provide enough water for the new locks. Just over the last hill, giant construction cranes come into view putting the final touches on the new canal. To starboard is Fort Sherman. Yes, that U.S. general. who happened to cross here in the late 1840's by foot, long before the Canal.

We step down three more locks in about two hours and glide out into Colon Bay, named for Columbus.

Looking back at the Isthmus I still cannot contemplate how anyone could even dream, let alone build a canal over those mountains and through that jungle. A land divided, a world united for 100 years.

Happy Birthday Panama Canal, and many more!

Heading north through the Canal

PANAMA CANAL ITINERARY

Print Luggage Tags Here.

Second Panama Cruise

SHIP NAME	SAILING DATE	STATEROOM	BOOKED BY
Norwegian Jewel	11/25/2016	4526 - FWD DECK 4	NCL MESA INBOUND

PIER ADDRESS

BOARDING PROCESS

•Boarding begins at 12:00 P.M.
Please note the time you have selected to arrive at the pier. Guests arriving to the pier before your select arrival time will be asked to come back at the appropriate time.

Save time by affixing these tags to your suitcases before arriving to the pier.

PORT OF CALL/ITINERARY	ARRIVE	DEPART
LOS ANGELES, CALIFORNIA, US	11/25/16 05:00	
AT SEA		
CABO SAN LUCAS, MEXICO	11/27/16 10:00 AM	11/27/16 06:00 PM
AT SEA		
ACAPULCO, MEXICO	11/29/16 08:00 AM	11/29/16 06:00 PM
AT SEA		
PUERTO QUETZAL, GUATEMALA	12/01/16 08:00 AM	12/01/16 06:00 PM
CORINTO, NICARAGUA PUNTARENAS,	12/02/16 08:00 AM	12/02/16 04:00 PM
COSTA RICA	12/03/16 08:00 AM	12/03/16 06:00 PM
AT SEA		
DAYLIGHT TRANSIT PANAMA CANAL	12/05/16 12:00 AM	12/05/16 12:00 AM
CARTAGENA, COLOMBIA, COLOMBIA	12/06/16 10:00 AM	12/06/16 06:00 PM
ATSEA		
AT SEA		
MIAMI, FLORIDA, US	12/09/16 08:00 AM	

Old Man and the Sea

An old man and the sea. Sixteen days at sea crossing through the Panama Canal and across the Caribbean leads one to paraphrase Hemingway. Up at 5:30 a.m., watching 965 feet of a 14-deck ship glide sideways to a pier without a bump still amazes me. Not a computer steering but a captain.

The NCL *Jewel* is the first ship to dock at the Port of Houston's new terminal. I watch a semi-truck pull up even before the line handlers finish their job. The truck is forced to back up several hundred feet—another amazing feat.

Past customs, we arrive on land and the rush of a New York traffic hour. (Okay, not that bad.) The gentleman next to me, from Alaska, is trying to have a relative pick him up at the terminal. Frustrated, he finally says, "I am standing right under the three flags! What do you mean you only see two? There are three!" I politely ask if his relative happens to be at the wharf in Galveston. He is, case solved, but the Alaskan is not a happy man! For two weeks, he had smiling crewmembers at his elbow answering every question and meeting every need—real or not. Reality can be so cruel.

Our cab arrives and we are off to Galveston, via Baybrook Mall to pick up more passengers. After fighting traffic, we arrive. Two young ladies squeeze in with more shopping bags than we have suitcases. The bags are from Victoria's Secret. My guess is that explains why they are at the mall. Probably can't buy those items in Walmart in Galveston.

"So glad you're here, we are running late," one of the young ladies shares with a South African accent. We learn they have to be back on their ship in 30 minutes to open the spa before sailing. The ship is 25 miles away. The cab driver made it with a few hints from me, an experienced commuter.

While the ships are incredible, the international crew and their lives are even more so. Cruise ships out of Galveston have over 900 hard working crewmembers each. Standing on the wharf you can see which of the lucky crew gets off for a few hours. They walk right past you texting at a blazing pace, never looking up, heading straight to Starbucks Wi-Fi, touching their children and families only though Skype. Remember to tip well.

If you can climb ten stories of stairs, repeatedly, take the behind the scenes ship tour. My favorite is the *Triumph*. Behind the crew-only doors is an understanding of their world. This is where the crew lives in stark white metal for nine months straight, 24/7.

On the lowest decks, the crew cabins are like small, built-in dorm rooms—neatness is a necessity. There is a cafeteria and a pub. Also, a small computerized school to help with language skills (something I could use),career advancement and human resources issues. Crewmembers must wear their nametags and maintain a professional relationship with passengers at all times.

Think of the complexity of a ship. A self-contained vast hotel in a totally self-sufficient town of 5,000 folks. Doctors, sales staff, waiters, police, cabin attendants (magic how the cabin is straightened up every time you leave—how do they do that?) mechanics, and more.

When the ship docks, people, fuel, food and luggage, are loaded and then gone in just a few hours, along with so many wharf tales.

Note: After two years, the beautiful Houston Passenger Terminal was closed due to delays caused by fog.

Silver mules position a break bulk vessel in lock

Chapter 7 - Caribbean, including Cuba

My Ship Just Came in, So I'm Gone

Sitting on the dock at Fisherman's Wharf I am often focused on the *Elissa's* dingy gently rocking-reflecting her oar's pulls of days gone past. A few years ago, small boats, lighters, ferried cargo back and forth to sailing ships anchored in deeper water.

Today cruise ships *Freedom* and *Triumph* are tied up at concrete docks, semi-trucks deliver the goods. How does this work, I wondered?

I was to board the *Triumph* for a 22-day voyage. So, with Ted O'Rourke's guidance I did a behind the scenes tour just to be sure there were enough supplies for three weeks at sea.

As we walked up to Terminal One, the largest single ship terminal in the world, the usual controlled chaos confronted us. Of course, to "turn" large ships with thousands of passengers there is a method and coordination.

Small forklifts rushed into 55-foot trailers, backed out, spun around and zipped into the terminal dropping the pallet in one of several rows, as directed by a young second generation union African-American man.

Other forklifts grabbed the pallet and with a yell, a Carnival cruise ship woman employee told them which ship door to take it to, while checking each off on her clipboard. Off rushed kegs, tissue, ice cream, Guy's Burgers, fruit, steaks, and my favorite, lobster, to the ship.

Strolling to the east end of the terminal, we saw tons of suitcases on trolleys rolling into the vast terminal. Let's just say I never heard any cruise ship passenger say, "I didn't bring enough clothes." As we walked past the luggage racks piled high as small houses I can see why.

Hawaiian-shirt-wearing International Longshoremen Associate (ILA) members working weekends for extra wages pushed the carts. Mr. Lloyd George from the banana warehouse was by the break room organizing everything.

Carts are wheeled up to x-ray machines, just like at the airport; each bag is placed on the belt and checked by a TSA agent. Once cleared they are picked up by young union workers and put in large containers on pallets. More forklifts hurry these on the ship. Sorted by deck, the bags are delivered to each cabin, sometimes by small but strong Filipino women. Not sure how they do it. All the passengers have to do is somehow lift their suitcase onto the bed, ugh.

Only the ship's size and use of forklifts seems to have changed through the ages. Human labor and knowledge of the loading process are so necessary even today. Most workers shared a big smile in the maze of hamburgers and suitcases.

Time to rush home and finish packing. One bag for shoes, formal, running, sandals, flip-flops and socks from Tri Fit. Backpack for medicine. Briefcase with the manuscript for revision of a book I co-authored with my brother of *60 Minutes* fame. Tuxedo bag Cruz found for me. Huge suitcase for everything else.

Here is where we are going on the Caribbean Sea trip for 22 days, leaving Jan. 16, 2016: Galveston, Grand Cayman, Aruba, Bonaire, Grenada, Martinique, St. Maarten, Puerto Rico, St. Thomas, St. Kitts, St. Martin, Antiqua, Grand Turk, Half Moon Cay, within five miles of Miami, and back to Galveston.

Now where is my passport?

On Board Ship and Ready to Sail South

It is like returning to a place you used to live, cozy and familiar. Yet the ship is larger than any Houston skyscraper. Walk up the ramp, hand your card to the smiling security woman and you step into luxury. This is the cruise ship, *Carnival Triumph*, home again, this time for 22 days.

Letting the nice young man on the phone in Miami choose the cabin location saved lots of money. For someone who doesn't gamble—I taught statistics after all—this time it really paid off.

The cabin is next to the forward elevator; deck one, only fifteen feet above the water. I sleep right next to the window—Okay, large porthole. It is like being a third of the way up the mast of the *Elissa*. Perfect.

Out the window I have a front row seat, watching the final acts of loading suitcases and food. Last minute scurrying, the Brinks money truck backs away, having loaded lots of cash I hope. Then the passenger walkway draws back, leaving only the crew's gangplank. Right below are four blue water hoses running from a huge faucet into the ship. A ballet begins with eight men rolling the pipes up and packing the supports. This process is repeated at each port.

Each man has a series of tasks they perform on cue. Quite a show.

The cabin is rather large, containing the bed, and a full-size couch. Another bed can drop from the ceiling for a fourth person. That might be crowded. One wall—bulkhead—has a counter, drawers and closets. A wall long mirror helps enlarge the space. Everything fits, even tons of luggage—suitcases under the bed, good to go.

At the Purser desk a guest is angrily complaining that her suitcase with her life-saving medicine is not here yet. We haven't even left yet. Cruise lines tell you not to pack your meds. The purser, Miljana, from Serbia, listens as the complaint is repeated over and over. When the woman comes up for air, Miljana lists three options—my option is put the woman off the ship. By now the line is very long and I have learned the life story of the folks behind me.

Later I tell Miljana how well I thought she handled the situation. Come to find out, the suitcase had been delivered to the woman's cabin, but she hadn't looked. I wonder what real horrors Miljana must have faced growing up in Serbia.

Wandering around as it begins to rain I am glad that the aft pool has a cover. It has turned cold. Yuck. South American will be warm, I hope.

Time for supper, including introductions of my fellow diners. Wonderwhere they are from? "World famous Pendleton, "Texas"—where? "Houston," in the beltway? "League City." "You know where that is?" Yes, I live in the same county. And on it goes, a fun time for all. The staff is from Peru, Budapest, and China. The world begins to expand as we set sail.

Time to head south. Next stop Aruba, 26 miles from Venezuela.

Loud, Rude and Proud of It

"'Abomination, you mean," a heavyset man in the front of the van cries out in a thick Texas accent referring to President Obama. Others mumbled more negative comments. I cringe.

This is not the first time a "Texan" displayed rude manners on this cruise. Loud and in your face seems to give these large white men a kick of adrenaline, shaming the other 1000+ Texans on board. I resort to "I am from Galveston, somewhere near Texas."

Our guide, Joe, had just proudly announced that in 2008, Antigua had renamed the tallest mountain Mount Obama in recognition of the United States' first black president. Joe is a thin young man with long braided hair and very black skin. As found on other Caribbean islands, he is very proud of the island's young democracy. Most Caribbean countries have been free for only three decades.

'Discovered' by Columbus during one of his four voyages, European powers soon wiped out the native Caribe population, bringing thousands of slaves through the triangle trade. On each island the tour guide, almost always a descendant of slaves, credits the French, British, Dutch or Spanish with building this or that. Politely I inquire if, indeed, it was the slaves who actually built it. Like our U.S. Capitol.

"Yes," they answer, with a slight twinkle in their eyes. A small crack in the mask they must wear.

The history of the windward volcanic islands is slave-intensive labor providing sugar cane production. Some ports, like San Juan, constructed massive forts dug by more slaves to protect the wealth stolen from South America by Spain.

Slaves were freed here in the 1830's, long before the U.S., yet the islands were still colonies for another 150 years. Seems that once all the juice was squeezed out of each island it was turned over to the descendants of the slaves.

Now tourists make snide remarks about the "poverty" islanders live in. Really? Let me take you to a few places in Texas.

The morning after the Iowa caucuses, our guide, Mr. Roland Hall, explains in detail the results and implications. I doubt if many of us know where Grand Turk is; fewer still know about its election process. The only connection perhaps is that on Grand Turk LBJ (a Texan, as I recall), welcomed John Glenn back from space.

On the way back from the beach I said that I enjoyed swimming in the Caribbean. Mr. Hall responded that I had been in the Atlantic: Grand Turk is north of the Caribbean. A common mistake, he graciously adds.

Mr. Hall is a middle-aged descendant of slaves. His university degrees are in English and Geography. He teaches and does tours to supplement his pay. Sounds like U.S. teachers working at Walmart after hours.

Clearly a well-educated man of the world, Mr. Hall, like most Caribbean folks, knows much more about us than we do about the world outside the U.S. or even Texas. Maybe instead of insulting each other overseas, we could listen. It might be polite and certainly more useful in making friends.

Admiral Lord Horatio Nelson's Dockyard Antigua, 1787

"Boom," the cannon fires from the fort atop a rock cliff. The 18th century man-of-war runs up the correct signal flag code. In a few moments the ship begins to lower sails as it is allowed entrance through the narrow opening to the small bay.

Lowering more sails, the ship drifts by Admiral Lord Horatio Nelson's flagship. He lives aboard rather than on land during his three-year tenure here.

Later that week, at low tide, the ship is careened, that is rolled on its side on the sandy beach. Three large capstans and strong backs are used in this feat. Sailors scrape the barnacles off, repaint the bottom and replace copper plates.

Nelson's Dockyard is on Antigua, an island on the northeast shoulder of the Caribbean. This leeward island is a great location to keep an eye on the French on Guadeloupe. It's the center of all the pirates and naval action for two centuries. Columbus did a sail-by in 1493 (second trip) waking the local Caribe's, I am sure.

The dock's site is the setting for hundreds of historical and fictional books. Each creates a romantic time of sail and courage.

This morning, sitting at my favorite table high up on the modern-day cruise ship *Triumph*'s deck, I can almost touch the stone walls of the fort. This is what I came to see. Unlike some famous places—we all know which ones—this one is not a disappointment. This one is better than anticipated.

The harbor is snug, much smaller than one would imagine. Ships backthen were about one-tenth as large as they are now. Galveston's *Elissa* next to the *Liberty* gives you an idea.

Stepping out of the bus, Joe, our guide, gives us 45 minutes to explore the dock with a tour group. I wander off. The harbor is fully restored to its 1783 glory; only now world-class racing sailboats tie up here. The brick sail shop, carpenters' sheds and blacksmith furnace are all here wrapped with bright tropical flowers. A house full of ship's figureheads as works of art. Walking the cobble stone streets it is easy to be transported back to the ship's stores and the officer's quarters of Nelson's time.

Books with words of brilliance are wonderful transportation to the past; but still not quite being there. Pictures are worth a thousand words, yet seen in person, breathing, smelling and touching is priceless. Back on board, my newest Dudley Pope's Lord Ramage novel of the 18th century Navy comes to life like never before.

Tiny Little's Rowboat Adventure Across the Sea

Antigua's Lord Nelson's dock on a Caribbean dry 85-degree day. We are surrounded by tropical flora, both through sight and smell. Walking up under a reconstructed 18th century porch designed to store massive masts, I spy a very fragile looking twenty-one-foot long contraption covered with decals. It is a rowboat, the Womble. There are a set of oars, a seat and a cabin, the size of a pup tent. Then I remember. James (Tiny) Little rowed this boat alone across the Atlantic in 116 days.

Other cruise ship passengers begin to gather. I tell them the story. Comments include "What a nut." "How stupid." "Idiotic." "Didn't he have something better to do?" The cruisers shuffle off to gawk at something else.

Continuing to examine the boat, I answer to myself. "Well, Tiny could have been on a cruise ship stuffing his face, raising his blood pressure and making judgmental statements."

What drove this man to make this unusual trip? After all, even Columbus and the Vikings had sails.

Tiny opened a pub in England after serving in the British Navy for fourteen years. Colin Davenport, who was a regular at the pub, lost his 17-year-old son to suicide in 2003. Tiny had two teenagers, so it hit him hard. He found no suicide prevention programs. Tiny decided to raise funds for a charity.

His method was to promise to row from the Canary Islands to Antigua, 3,489 miles. For months, he trained, losing weight and fine-tuning his stroke. A video diary of his trip (You Tube: *The Ocean Rowers, Tiny Little*) reveals how he kept sane, sort of. One day he saw a large tanker heading right toward the Womble. Radioing the captain, he said he was right in front of the captain's ship, rowing across the ocean. The captain's reply was, "Are you nuts?" Tiny responded, "Yes, probably."

He rowed thirty miles, fourteen hours per day. Day after day after day.

The next morning, I head for the cruise ship's gym and get on the rowing machine. Eleven decks up it faces an expansive view of the ocean. Some days I row, thoughts tumbling through my mind. Other days I visit with whomever is on the other machine. After each 20-minute session in the air-conditioned gym, no salty waves breaking over me, I am in awe and raise my water bottle to the 49-year-old Tiny. "Cheers to you, sir, and your cause."

Tiny Little's row boat

The Devil's Guard Post in Old San Juan

The fog flows through the early morning air, waves crashing below, only heard, not seen. A guard stands alone shivering in the 'guerita', the small round lookout. Built at the point of a triangular mini fort, the structure is just large enough for one soldier. He looks out through slots built into the stone wall covered by a dome. The year is 1670.

Later that morning, the guard's replacement yells out. Hearing no reply, he draws his sword and approaches with caution. Peering in the door he sees only the guards uniform in a heap on the floor. He cries out to the other soldiers above in the main part of the fort. They come running down to witness the disappearance themselves. The 'capitan' calmly explains to the men at muster that the guard was taken by the devil as punishment for deserting his post. "Let this be a lesson," he warns. "Stay at your post, or El Diablo will carry you away to your death."

Ranger Silva finishes the story. "May I go down to the 'guerita'?" I venture. "No, I am sorry it is closed to the public," he replies. "But you can go down several flights of stone steps, walk out to the point and look down at the guerita." I am out the door headed that way almost before he finishes. What amazing places, Castillo San Cristobal and the more famous sister fort, El Morro are—even better than the pictures. Covering almost 100 acres between them they tower above Old San Juan, Puerto Rico, on a hill overlooking the ocean on the back side.

Exiting the ship that morning, I thought I would walk to them. Wondering where they were, I was looking at one of the huge rock walls but didn't know it. I asked a couple walking down the wharf if they knew where the fort could be found. The gentleman began to explain, and realizing it was getting very confusing, asked if I wanted a ride. After a drive through narrow twisting cobblestone streets we came to a huge lawn laid out before El Morro. The couple was living in San Juan while their daughter did her Coast Guard tour. Nice folks.

Beginning in 1539, the forts protected the San Juan harbor, a safe haven for Spanish galleons between South America and Spain. Sir Francis Drake was defeated here in 1595 as were other English attempts. From 1765-1783 under the direction of Tomas O'Daly, an Irishman, the Spanish built the forts—the best in the world. In 1898, after the Spanish-American war, Puerto Rico became part of the U.S.A. Therefore, my National Parks Senior Pass gains me free entrance and access to Ranger Silva's expertise and wonderful story-telling.

The real story, Ranger Silva divulged, was that the guard swam away to elope with the general's daughter, not the devil. To keep the rest of the soldiers in line, under terrible living circumstances, the 'capitan' made up the story. In the 1600's people believed in myths, so it worked. Actually, myths still work today. After all, it is the political season.

San Juan Guard House

Puerto Rico's Evita on Columbus Square

"In a nutshell, it's a plaza to commemorate the "discoverer" of the Americas. There's not really much to do aside from snapping photos of the statue or of yourself." So writes "garridogal" on a webpage. Let me tell you another story of Plaza de Colon, Columbus Square, San Juan, Puerto Rico.

On the edge of Old San Juan, with the tall Columbus statue, and the fountain under the old large trees, in my mind, the square oozes Spain. Surrounding the plaza are booths selling homemade soaps, jewelry, carvings and woven dolls. Interacting with the husband or the women who created the products is a special treat.

A Puerto Rican food truck produced a delicious native dish—like so many tasty recipes I am not sure of the ingredients. The mango juice was so cool and refreshing, like this with al fresco dining. Time to explore the stone-front stores lining the square.

The century old cobblestone pavement massaged my feet through the soles of my sandals. Known as Adoquines, the stones form azul (blue) lines in the road. The bricks were made from slag left in the bottom of the furnace. Thought of as worthless, the stones were used as ballast on Spanish ships. In 1600 San Juan, they became valuable.

Entering an avant-garde artsy shop, I am overwhelmed by the blend of modern and native handcrafts. Sensing my confusion, Evita, an eye-catching and engaging sales woman with lustrous silver hair, asks, "May I interest you in something?" She gently touches my elbow and speaks articulately in an accent that is heavy—Castilian to my tin ear.

After my weak joke about "Don't fear for me Argentina," I inquire regarding the source of a Mardi Gras style mask. "Martinique," she replies, touching my arm in a common Latin American fashion. "Oh," I reply. "I was just there. They appeared unfriendly and only spoke French, which for folks whose main income is from English-speaking U.S. cruise ship passengers did not compute." She explained they are descended from slaves and the country is still poor. They are unhappy people," she summarized.

"I want to thank you for speaking English so well. Sorry my Spanish isn't better," I said.

Laughing she replied, "That is sweet, but I am from the Bronx, New York City. I moved back to care for my mother."

Everyone here seems to work hard and cares for each other, particularly family. Too bad the country is going bankrupt. Strange, the U.S. Congress decides Puerto Rico's fate when there are no congresspeople allowed from here. Some signs in San Juan read, "No taxation without representation." Like 1776 for the rest of us?

A little research reveals that U.S. hedge funds are on the hook for making questionable loans. Sound familiar? Sure enough, back home, ads begin running that "U.S. teachers will be harmed if Puerto Rico is allowed to go bankrupt." Actually, not rearranging their debt will result in cutting basic government services, and it's the hedge funds and international banks who will lose.

We have closer ties to this Island than most of us know, unless you are from the Bronx.

El Faro, Crooked Island, Bahamas, and a Hurricane

El Faro has been on my mind since hearing of its sinking during Hurricane Joaquin last October off Crooked Island, the Bahamas. *El Faro*, 800-foot cargo ship was just like the ones motoring down the Houston channel every day. All thirty-three U.S. crew were lost at sea. Sad, but soon forgotten.

Except this time. Crooked Island rings a bell. It is the home of Fritz Damler and Mari Anderson. Their wonderful book, *Plunge* (Amazon), details building their beachfront home. Last month when eating lunch with the couple in New Mexico, I carefully raised the question regarding hurricane damage.

Fritz summed it up. "All low-lying areas of the island were inundated with up to eight feet of saltwater, roads and utilities wiped out. Homes were flooded, destroying appliances and vehicles. Our home fared pretty well with mostly wind damage to roofing and windows. The garage roof flew a quarter-mile down the beach and augured into a sandy bluff but the contents of said garage were spared. Fortunately, there was no loss of life. We're heading down in January to make repairs."

As only a landlubber and cruise ship rider, I was not familiar with Crooked Island. It sounded exotic and way off the beaten, or sailed, path. Come to find out, just thirty-five miles off-shore is a busy shipping route, Florida to the Eastern Caribbean. This is the course Capt. Michael Davidson chose trying to miss the predicted northern path of Joaquin. As Galvestonians know, hurricanes have minds of their own, as Joaquin did, heading south before hooking north.

Waves rose to mountains. CBS's *60 Minutes* reports engine power was lost, probably causing the ship to broach, turning sideways to the waves. Without propulsion, the ship was at the mercy of the sea. The top two decks of the aft "skyscraper" were torn off, including the bridge with the captain. When visiting the port, see how high up this is on a ship. The waves' size and supremacy are difficult to imagine.

See a fully enclosed orange lifeboat on the ship? The 40-year-old *El Faro* was grandparented-in—open lifeboats were allowed. One boat was found, empty. Not a fair fight trying to survive in 140 mph sustained wind-whipped seas.

El Faro now sits upright 15,000 feet deep off Crooked Island, deeper than Titanic. The orange "black box" was found over a year later on the third try. It revealed the last 26 hours of the crew's actions and fears as the ship came apart. Old equipment, outdated data and failing to change course sealed the ship and crew's fate. The last words: "I'm not leavin' you, let's go," the captain loudly responded to the helmsman.

Now we know what husbands, wives, new dads, brothers, daughters, and sons faced before their deaths. What was the rush to get to Puerto Rico? Why risk sailing into a hurricane? We don't know for sure yet. One relative concluded the answer was to get frozen chicken there fast. Greed?

What a high cost. Thirty-three American seafarers lost off Crooked Island. CNN said using an old law, the ship owners have already sued to limit possible claims of the families. What future will their children, siblings and parents experience without them? Victims of more greed?

Container ship loading in Cartagena

Caribbean Sea Memories

"Oh, shucks." The false-dawn light seeps around the curtain. Time to get up and stumble aft to the coffee up on the cruise ship's Lido Deck Nine. It has been a delightful 22 days living on the Riviera—deck that is, also known as Deck One.

As we enter the channel, I can see the lights of Galveston and the proud bows of USS *Stewart* and USS *Cavalla*, still on guard. Where did the time go?

Memories emerge from the fog in my mind. Swimming at Grand Cayman's Seven-mile Beach after touring the town of Hell. Discussions of offshore banking with local folks.

Bright Dutch-style homes in the perfectly dry weather of barren Aruba. Eating grilled grouper on the beach, only 26 miles from Venezuela.

The diving capital of Bonaire, offered only dead coral off the beach at a 'resort'. Grenada, by contrast was lush with spices, waterfalls, white beaches and history. Dancing with a local band. Walking up a steep hill with my new friend-of-a-friend, Steve, we discovered the site of the last stand of the dictator in 1983. The US Marines took over this stone fort, liberating the Grenada people. Or so I am told.

Martinique is a beautiful Strand-style island with very unhappy French-speaking people. A perception based only on fellow passengers' and my experiences.

St. Maarten for spring break at Maho Beach where the huge airplanes skim over bikini-clad partyers at the end of the runway. It's a steep rough beach; I have a hole in my foot to prove it. Returning a few days later, I venture to the calmer French side with fantastic cliff-side views of the Atlantic.

In 1917 for only $25M, the U.S. purchased the Virgin Islands. We got a super deal. My goal of swimming on every island is thwarted on St. John's. The bus driver was unconvinced to stop in the National Park at the most perfect beaches on the trip. I will return, backpack and sleeping bag in tow.

A tour of St. Kitts, home to Thomas Jefferson's grandfather, provided Tahiti-type views of Nevis, the birthplace of Alexander Hamilton. Antigua and Grand Turk warranted their own columns.

Half Moon Cay in the Bahamas is inhabited by only a watchman, until the ship arrives pouring 2,000 passengers onto the pure white beach. As I swam out a third of a mile, all I could see was brilliant white sand twelve feet below. When we left that evening, a lone sailboat glided up to anchor. Diving for lobster for dinner, that is the life.

The next morning, I plainly see the beautiful beach skyline of Miami. The captain announces we are transferring a passenger to a fireboat for medical reasons.

Next port, Galveston. The *Triumph* leaves this afternoon for a seven-day voyage to Jamaica. Can I stay on? Six thousand miles wasn't enough. Now back to reality, doing the laundry and making my own bed, all with Caribbean Sea memories.

Freedom Found: A Cuban Raft Refugee Story

A pleasing early fall Saturday evening on 23rd Street, my favorite block. At Postoffice Street a poster invites me into Affaire d' Art Gallery to view the Cuban Refugee raft. Great, I've wanted to see it all summer.

The next exciting "find" is Maureen "Mo" Huddleston, the artist who brought the raft to the public from a lonely Gulf beach. This determined woman researched and rescued the raft, with a team of volunteers. I want to talk about the raft, she wants to know if I will help move it to The Market Place at the Peanut Butter Warehouse.

The next day I show up ready to go. With anthropologically informed precision she directs the packing of the numerous items found on the raft, from blocks of rice to black shoes and gloves. The next day as we reassemble the raft, I am struck with a powerful feeling. A real person, who probably perished, held dreams of a better life and gripped the tree branch tiller handle I now hold.

What drives men, women and children to climb on a raft of Styrofoam, logs and rebar? What policies and political platitudes drive them? From Columbus in 1492, to slaves, to mafia-run casinos and U.S. corporate plantations in the 1950s, the Cuban people have suffered and hoped. With one U.S. backed dictator, Batista, replaced by the Russian supported Castro brothers, and a fifty-year embargo promoting only poverty, people continue to flee across the sea. Some make it with one dry foot. Some are intercepted by the Coast Guard and returned to Cuba. And others have died. Just like the Syrian raft refugees.

The signs on this raft tell of desperate measures, chopping down the mast, broken u-joint and no Coast Guard spray paint marks of rescue. Maybe up to fifteen people hung on to this 20x9-foot raft, the size of a cruise liner's cabin. Driven by Storm Bill, the raft failed to make the 100-mile journey to Florida, rather traveling 1,000 miles to our Texas beach.

Over the years I have known Cuba through books, our church-sponsored Cuban family, and my brother's church trip, 23 years ago. A wonderful day visiting with a Cuban doctor in the Belizean jungle provided more insight.

Cuba has a complex history and a complicated future. Just like the many items scattered across the freedom on a Styrofoam raft.

A Cuban Raft Rescue

Last June, Mo Huddelston found a Cuban refugee raft on Matagorda Beach and then put it on display. Saturday, we will celebrate the exhibit with Cuban food, music and artists. Hundreds of folks have seen the exhibit, and some have left notes. One note was from Mike and Janice Algermissen. They observed a similar raft last year. Their account with permission follows.

"Twenty-three miles off the coast of Mexico's Yucatan Peninsula, the *Caribbean Princess* made its scheduled turn heading south toward Roatan. A small boat three miles off port bow appeared. It was different from most fishing boats because of a makeshift sail. The captain slowly brought the ship close to the small raft, as the people stood and waved. Clearly, they were in distress and needed help. The man overboard crew approached the raft in the ship's rescue boat to establish communication.

These 12 people on board sailed from Cuba, fall of 2015, headed for Progresso, Mexico. Several days later, the little motor caught fire and was destroyed. They tried to fashion a sail but it was of little help. The homemade craft, caught in the "Yucatan Loop", drifted until spotted by the ship.

The ship's medical team went to the raft and checked the passengers' health. They appeared healthy but were thirsty and hungry. The *Caribbean Princess* sent over food and water. The captain called the Mexican Coast Guard and told them the ship would stay with the raft until they arrived. Two hours later the Mexican Coast Guard came and loaded the Cubans on board. The *Caribbean Princess* proceeded towards Roatan. The raft was left adrift in the Yucatan channel."

As Scott Beyer writes in the March 4, 2016, issue of Forbes magazine, "balseros", the Cuban raft refugees, face many challenges on the homemade rafts. Any waves over ten feet can sink the Styrofoam rafts. Dehydrated, soaked by the sea, hypothermia can cause hallucinations. Sharks may attack passengers when they go to the bathroom over the side.

Luis Albelo sailed from Cuba to south of Miami on a raft years ago. Now he travels to Cuba regularly to visit his daughter. One of Fidel Castro's greatest fears was American tourists. Cruise ships are ready to flood the island nation with tourists. Then hopefully, no more rafts will be necessary for Cubans to experience freedom.

Cuban raft rescue by Mexican Coast Guard

Photo by Mike Algermissen

Matters of the Sea - Cuba

Walking in the front door after another October day in seventh grade, I sensed my usually calm mother's anxiety. Something was different. It was Oct. 1962, the tense days of near total destruction of the U.S.A. and Russia, not to mention Cuba. After all, she had four boys and we lived near a mountain full of atomic bombs in New Mexico. My father was on active duty on a destroyer near Key West. Uncle Wally, captain of a submarine, was preparing to land SEALs on a beach in Cuba. Aunt Susie and my four cousins were playing on the anti-tank structures on a Key West beach. The adults all held their breath for 12 days until the Russian ships turned around and sailed back across the sea. For most of my youth, I was told Cuba was evil. Once I began to read history, I found there was more to the story. The

Mafia ruled casinos and U.S. companies exploited many Cubans. Then Castro's righteous revolution turned to more of the same abuse.

My brother visited Cuba 25 years ago through a church group. Working in Belize, I met Cuban doctors and Olympic athletes doing anti-drug programs with kids. On cruise ships, I sailed all the way around the island, home of 11 million who were by our standards, poor but healthy people. Standing in Key West, I stare south trying to see across the ninety miles—Galveston to Conroe. So close, yet so divided, so deadly for those in small boats, reaching for one foot on dry land.

Now, after fifty years, Richard Blanco has put into striking words the pain, the sameness and the hope of bringing us together. These are some of the phrases from his poem, which settled in my mind. My sincere apologies to the author for any misquote. See the internet for his reading of the full poem.

Matters of the Sea, Cosas del Mar. Read at the opening of the U.S. Embassy in Havana, 2015.

"The sea doesn't matter, what matters is this: We all belong to the sea between us."

"... the child ... who sculptures dreams into impossible castles"

"... strolling down either shore, our footprints vanish in the waves ..., home to all of our silent wishes"

"... our grandfathers ... planting maple or mango trees, which outlive them. Our mothers teaching us how to read in Spanish or English, how to tie our shoes ..."

" ... we all walk barefoot and bare soul among the soars and dives of seagull cries."

" ... we have all cupped seashells up to our ears to listen again to the echo."

"... today the sea still telling us the end to all our doubts and fears is to gaze into the lucid blues of our shared horizon, to breathe together, to heal together."

Thank you, Richard Blanco, for your words. Now I can see better across the sea, too. And Mother is calm, at least about Cuba.

Havana and the Cuban capitol through the morning air

Our Man in Havana

A small paved parking lot surrounded by thousands of Italian marble sculptures marks where Christopher Columbus, who "discovered" Cuba, was to be buried. The Spanish of course reneged on the agreement. Welcome to Havana.

I am standing in the 500-year-old city cemetery, now home to two million dead Spanish and Cubans who are buried here, in a city which is home to two million very alive Cubans.

My father's Navy tales of Cuba of the 1950s and my brother's visit 25 years ago sparked a desire to visit this amazing country. This longtime dream was finally being realized.

Only two steps off the ship's gangway I passed back

through centuries of colonialism, capitalism and communism. I had planned to come on the new wave of Obama's openness. Now I am here, just before the door slams shut again.

Earlier this morning, the small TV in our cabin revealed a thin line of lights on the dark gray screen. Up to the 11th deck, no oatmeal, okay, fruit will do, and coffee. Awake as the ship slipped down the narrow entrance canal almost to USS *Maine's* 1898 anchorage in Havana's small bay. I see a slight glow behind a giant 70-foot-tall bright white statue of Jesus, Cuba's Christ, standing next to the largest stone fortress in the New World. Bow in at the San Francisco wharf. Welcome to Cuba.

"Albin? Albin?" Here is Roderigo's representative, our guide, Lou, and Julio, the driver of our sort of 1956 Cadillac. As the grandson of Chevrolet Charlie, I know every year and model of 1950-1968 American made cars. This is great.

The Cuban car versions are produced by the world's best mechanics, ours with a Perkins diesel engine, tractor transmission and topless. No *Coast Monthly* car stories here, still stories to be sure.

Lou is a Sandy Koufax look-alike who later showed me the grips he used when pitching semi-pro, which is saying something in Cuba. Julio is a Richard Gere look-alike.

Off we roar, coughing diesel fumes through all of old Habana, on the Malecon, Havana's version of our seawall, "Miamitized". Thirty-foot waves from hurricanes have battered the lower floors of the centuries old buildings. Upper floors reveal the romantic past. As Cuban architect Eusebio Leal said, "Everyone agrees it's a city covered in a veil of nostalgia, of crumbling decadence."

Standing on the seawall serious fishermen cast into the straits of Florida as white waves cascade into the street. History, sizzling sounds, art, food, sports, architecture and the people seep into one's senses.

Small parks, statues of heroes and 1950's-style buildings appear further down, including the Riviera Hotel. On a rock outcropping is the National Hotel, the Galvez of Cuba.

This is where in the 1940s the U.S. Mob planned its takeover of Cuba through gambling, the sex trade and anything you wanted until 1959. Then the mobsters ran for their lives back to Miami and Las Vegas. The National Hotel remains beautiful and restored. Welcome to Cuba.

Havana's ornate city cemetery

Cruising Around Cuba

Chauffeured down Cuba A-1, 10 lanes-wide, a 270-mile highway to nowhere. No traffic.

"Can you believe this highway was built for the military?" Lou asked.

"So was our freeway system," I replied.

We are headed to Finca Vigia, the lookout, Mary Hemingway's home and Ernest's workplace. Built on an old fort outside of Havana on a hilltop, it still offers splendid vistas. The best view is from the fourth story office where Hemingway wrote *The Old Man and the Sea*. His handsome, often-used boat, *Pilar*, rests below by the pool.

The home's bright white walled rooms are minimally decorated with symbols of his life. Each room roped off. As I began shooting photos through the doorway of his office, an attractive uniformed docent quietly approached, "Would you like me to take some pictures?"

Slipping her my camera, I said, "Gracias." Expertly framing each shot she returned within a minute.

"Do you have a little something for me?" she asked. I shook her hand with a $3 Cuban bill. Her eyes spoke. The photos were certainly worth the money, not to mention the seductive smile.

Cuba is held together by its people, their pride, resiliency and ingenuity; there is no other option. Christopher Columbus in 1492 described the inhabitants as "the best people in the world." Twenty years later the Spanish returned. Greeted by 3,000 cheerful Tianos, the Spanish slaughtered them. Then things got worse.

After murdering or working to death the rest of the natives, Spain turned to Africa for slaves whose average life lasted only seven years in Cuba. A hundred years of rebellion in the 1800s brought freedom in 1902 with an amendment to the new constitution. Cuba could do little without the approval of the good ole' U.S.A.

Another revolution headed by an attorney with guns and guts, Castro, kicked out the mob and their front man, Batista, in 1959.

Grabbing Soviet Russia as a surrogate big brother, Cuba stretched its hands throughout the world while driving the Miami mob and U.S. Presidents mad. When big brother collapsed in 1990, Cuba was economically battered but glad to see the Soviets depart. China provided one million bicycles and little else.

New government programs, a bit of health-related tourism and the Pan American games began to improve the economy. Olympic athletes inspired in Cuba and throughout the Caribbean.

The thing Fidel Castro feared the most, tourists, began to arrive. As Insight Guides-Cuba asks, "Tourism: Salvation or Sellout?" A truth, tourism with an underground market have become a commercial answer for the population.

During the 1990's, crumbling old Havana began to be slowly restored between hurricanes. The sports stadiums built for the games and entertainment were left to fall into ruin. Large fruit orchards and vegetable farms surrounding Havana were plowed under, replaced with coffee plants. These failed, producing a bitter taste in more ways than one.

As we pulled into the narrow streets of Cojimar I sensed "the old man and the sea", Gregorio Fuentes, the fisherman, in this timeworn angler's town. Across crumbled concrete was the wharf where Hemingway kept Pilar. To the left a short outlet to the wild sea.

One glance at the cramped craft shop and I wandered down a lonely 1930s street scene with a wayward puppy, until rescued by his master.

High noon and fish sounded good in this environ. A visit with several locals and we were off, up a hill to the most elegant car port ever.

Red-tiled roof over a wooden gate to tablecloths and uniformed wait staff. With drivers, guides and four tourists, we were eight. I picked up the tab for a three course, two-hour meal, drinks and 20% tip for $80 USD. No tourist trap here.

We drove back into Havana among the other stars of steel, past cars, past the ornate Ballet Nacional de Cuba, home of Alicia Alonso the mid-century prima ballerina with Balanchine. Surreal Cuba—literature, art, revolutions and pleasant folks.

Havana's Connection with Galveston

Lou, our guide, was excited. Wearing a 1940's style straw hat and shorts he shouted: "You're from Galveston? In the 1920s my grandfather used to go fishing for ten days out of Havana. Where he really went was to Galveston with a boat load of rum during Prohibition."

I explained that was part of our history and the makings of a famous family, the barber brothers turned entertainment masters, the Maceos. Their story was even made into a play. A relative, Tilman Fertitta, created a multibillion-dollar company including the Houston Rockets. "Wow, maybe we should've stayed in touch with them?" Lou responded.

I am not sure that would've done much good as many Cubans have not been allowed to travel outside their country during their whole life. Thus, the Cuban rafts we have found in the Gulf. Lou is a rare exception. As an economist, he worked for the government traveling to many countries negotiating contracts for Cuba.

As we toured the Castillo, I asked if he had ever seen the forts in Cartagena. "Oh yes," he said, and he'd been to Quito, Río de Janeiro and about five other major South American cities my ears could not keep up with. He knew his stuff. His stories rang true to me. Of course, I have only two trips to Colombia to go by.

Lou explained the demographics of Cuba. Considered a white Spanish gentleman, he said 60 percent of the country in 1960 was white, now down to about 37 percent. The largest group, is a blend of Spanish and African referred to as "mulatto", a term not always accepted in good company in the U.S. Eleven per cent are black.

The literacy rate among the 11 million Cubanos is 99 percent as reported by the CIA. Universal education.

Julio, our driver, has never been off the island. He'd like to visit new places. Manuel, another driver, is an Italian who chose to live in Cuba. His dark hair pulled back into a tight ponytail, mouth always with a smile, he's a hunk. While he travels routinely back to Italy he feels more comfortable in Havana than Rome.

Certainly, there is far less traffic here. Driving four days a week he is able to afford a comfortable high-rise apartment facing the sea. From a Syrian family, Jahlil, an English-speaking guide, was born here and never left, certainly not back to Syria. He would like to travel, but is not allowed.

Lou has two sons, both college-educated, an architect and a sports trainer. Neither can leave. They work for the government at about $20 a month plus free healthcare. Lou has big dreams for them.

We visited about families intermittently as we cruised through neighborhoods and alleyways accented with wires and poles, Galveston style. Otherwise the landscape was assessed through diesel haze of gray. Every mile or so a patch of green, a community park, a gathering place.

On these verde junctures Cubano eyes came alive, resiliency shone from the soul, insight decorated each statement, drowning out even a U.S. professor's knowledge of the past. The present is dismissed by "we have survived worse." Right now, we are all amigos in historical Havana.

Part of massive Spanish fort across from Havana

A Visit with Ché's Docent

As the ship guided through the narrow Canal de Entrada past the 1600's Castillo and mile-long Castillo De San Carlos, my focus was on a house with a red-tile roof. The fort's massive walls rise above a 100-foot cliff down to the sea.

The "new" fort was built in the late 1760's right after the British captured Havana. Within a year, the British returned

Cuba to Spain in exchange for Florida.

The new fort cost so much that the King of Spain declared that he should be able to see it from Madrid.

Centuries later at the Castillo, I left the tour group at the crafts booth and fast walked over drawbridges, two huge dry moats, up through two thick gates towards the channel. Four men up on a two-story scaffold chipped away at centuries old rock, never giving me a glance.

Ahead, I spied a sign pointing to the red-roofed Ché Guevara museum. Yet my mission was get to the wall for the view of Havana. This required going through the door. But it was blocked by a small, older, determined, fiesta-dressed Cuban woman. Her arm pointed to her left, right into the museum. Trapped, I replied "Buenas tardes, señora." In rapid Espanol, she effectively guided me to the first photo, Ché as a young doctor. I understood about 25 percent of her lecture, only because the captions were translated into English. I nodded, smiled and looked intently at the pictures.

I needed to let her know I was on a fast-paced tour. My broken Spanish resulted in her asking en Espanol, "Do you speak Spanish?"

My reply brought a sigh of almost disgust through her body language. That I understood.

I was rescued by her replacement. My docent split without even a look back. Not wanting to appear rude I stepped to the left—an escape route—right into Ché's personal office.

A small serene 8-by-15 room with undersized etched windows on the outer wall. A modest dark wooden desk stood at the far end with four matching chairs facing the desk. Only a blotter, pen set and pad. Prepared for an efficient process with no records. Quick "trials" took place here. Quietly my bones felt history was made in this office as Ché implemented the "revolution."

Batista's officers, found guilty, were marched down the path I had just followed to where firing squads shot them against the outer fortress wall. Bullet holes attest to the numbers.

"President" Batista, of course safely exited to the

Dominican Republic, his mob money in Switzerland. He left his giant Jesus and an economically drained country with a new dictator.

I ducked passed the new docent, and reached the wall to gaze down across at the magnificent vision of Havana without the detail of decay. The 500-year-old city to the right morphed into the 1920's era, D.C.-style capital seen just below the concrete tower on Revolution Square.

This is what I came for—history, views and, yes, even short visits with determined docents. I only regret I didn't tip her; she earned it.

Cuba and Getting in Line

People whisper propaganda; dictatorial decrees and corruption everywhere. The courts acquiesce.

Here I stand in a stark hall with 2,000 other folks, of all skin colorations, waiting on government officials to check our documents. All contacts and activities must be recorded and kept five years for government inspection.

For two hours, the line barely shuffled on the concrete floor. "Special" people allowed to take cuts. A uniformed official occasionally strolled by, hands behind his back, bearded face set in a stare.

Welcome back to the good old U.S.A. Our cruise ship staff had guided us into a disorganized standoff. Dragging our bags, we emerged into the humid heat of Miami having only been asked one question: my answer, "No."

Entering Cuba, it's simple, after completing U.S. paperwork, you walk off the ship, hand your U.S. passport to a customs agent who returns it within a few seconds with a smile.

There are lines in Cuba too. Up to fifty people, along Havana avenues every few blocks. They're waiting for buses or cabs or to buy food. No police, only self-regulated lines. The sound of a soft mechanical sounding wolf whistle occasionally radiates from 1950's American made cars. No loud horns. Once in a while the quiet is punctuated by a blast of Cubano music.

Color seems to have been bleached out of the city by 500 years of oppression, most recently the Soviet-gray apartment concrete boxes. The colorful Tropicana club does open every night for a crowd of tourists. A wonderful, live twelve-piece band plays for a couple of hours with tall beautiful women dancers, changing their skimpy feathered costumes every set. The rum flows, cigar smoke hangs low. Or so I am told. I chose not to participate in recreating the roaring post World War II mob-rule era.

Conversation with Cubans was of more interest to me. Their wishes, economics, the free market in Cuba and government policy. But not politics. I honored the tradition of not saying anything negative about our president on foreign soil. Something not respected by several older white males I witnessed during President Obama's term.

Openly criticizing their own government, Cubans pointed out flaws and lies. I was astonished at their unrestricted comments. Castro's name was not mentioned.

Cuba operates today on a parallel economic system. The official government: ration books, fixed pay, social services to all and limited private companies. There are taxi cabs, private cars and government vehicles which have B's on their license plates.

The other system is underground, with markets for everything. There was only one tourist trap. A car t-shirt was their last so they won't sell it to me—they need to work on that.

A Cuban economist told me the way to change their government was to totally lift the embargo; capitalism would swamp Cuba. "But it won't happen, the Miami Cuban mob is too comfortable in their U.S. paid beachfront offices," he said.

He ended by saying, "Oh, forget our governments; you and I can still be friends." Cuban truth.

Chapter 8 - Sailing

Twelve Metres of Thrill in Cozumel

Standing on the concrete wharf wearing my white Crew 12 shirt looking out over the Caribbean Sea. High noon, good time for a sail boat race. A shoot-out between two 1987 America's Cup Regatta boats, the *Stars and Stripes* (USA) and *True North IV* (Canada).

Soon we tourists are divided into two groups. Eight family members compose one crew; the remaining four of us the other. I hope for the *True North*, my winning boat. We get the *Stars*, my only loss. Asked our level of activity, three select watching. I volunteer for full. "This is going to be an embarrassing loss," I whisper to our CPA honorary captain. She chides, "Be positive." Aye.

Boarding, I don't see Ian, one of the brothers who captains each boat. He is helping his dad in Grenada. Gerry fills in. Tom captains *True North* for today's race. The brothers, born on a sailboat while their parents toured the world, are very competitive.

Three local staff join our boat, filling out the crew. Thanks to Pilates, I am the port aft grinder. Next, we are professionally trained, after all this is the actual challenge course in deep water.

The horn sounds and we are off, with *True* about 3 feet ahead. Tom shouts across the ten feet between the boats, "We are ahead." I yell back, "But we have your wind." Time to talk trash, like old salts. Well, at least I am old.

The race is a blur. We tack, jibe, over and over again. Working furiously and focused on my job, my only contact with the race is through Gerry's slight-accent commands and ongoing commentary.

Fast, running with the wind, deck at 45 degrees, he hops from the helm to the main grinder, "Alvin take the wheel." After past races, I was able to "steer" under calm conditions. Now I'm Dennis Connors under full sail. Wow, what a thrill ride. Wiping out visions of past capsizes, I brace and try to keep us from going over. The rule of ten and two never enters my mind.

A few minutes of blissful terror later, Gerry retakes the helm. The finish will be close; we need a puff of wind. We get it, winning by three feet. Back on the wharf, Tom and I hug, great competitor and friend. And I won.

It's the People, not the Sailboat - Capt. Mike

From crewing on the small Sonar sailboat for three races I knew this man had passion and no time for idle talk. So, I scheduled a meeting to find the passion's source.

Captain Mike Janota returned to Galveston Island as a newly minted college graduate in 1978 to begin his teaching career at O'Connell school. In addition to knowledge of history and social studies, he brought years of self-taught sail boating skills.

Before long he was crewing on Harris Kempner's boat. And winning. During a storm, the wealthy Kempner sat in the cockpit, tiller in hand when a huge wave knocked him into the cabin. Hurt, he climbed back to his place and joked "may need a life jacket." He steered for four more hours.

Racing weekly, sometimes they were short a crewmember. Captain Mike invited some of his eighth-grade students along. Soon they had both sailing know-how and the admiration of Mr. Kempner. He always took an interest in them, seeking their views on history, literature and current affairs. The students acquired more than sailing experience.

Capt. Mike's informal youth program grew into a non-profit by 1985 with 21 boats. The "Kempner kids" won regional regattas including the Bud Smith Trophy over much better funded teams.

September 2008, Hurricane *Ike* took it all: 21 boats, the marina, even Capt. Mike's home. He rolled up his sleeves and eight months later began rebuilding the sailing program focused on youth who needed a bit of guidance.

On the wharf one day Capt. Mike met Charles Doolin, who had a vision of creating a National Youth Community Sailing Center. Together the program now has 40 boats within a multimillion-dollar facility, Sea Star Base Galveston. College students from Boston to southern California come here to compete. Retirees to kids learn to sail and much more, like how to treat everyone with respect and dignity. Mr. Kempner would be proud; perhaps this is the best inheritance he could pass on to Capt. Mike.

On my first outing Capt. Mike asked me to help a tentative 14-year-old boy take the helm. We both discovered a great deal trying to steer a steady course. Sailing is the vehicle used to guide youth. Under Capt. David Gaston's Adaptive Sailing program, persons with disabilities, including wounded veterans, enjoy the sport, too. Captain Mike's boating clearly builds relationships, while bridging generations.

To get involved contact: www.SSBGalveston.org

Sailboat racing with the wind

Pillow Talk to Pirates

"You can't cross the sea staring at the water." Written on a throw pillow down on The Strand in the Admiralty storefront, the saying gives me pause. Okay, how can I get on the water today? A flyer nearby provides the answer: Capt. Kidd sunset evening sailing cruise. www.captkiddcharters.com.

A quick trip up Highway 146 to Kemah, a visit to the Eagle Nest store, source of my Pelican fan, a Vietnamese sandwich, a creamery ice cream, and I am ready to go.

Strolling down the yacht wharf past inviting million-dollar looking mini-cruise ships I spy a worn pirate flag on a 55-foot 19th century style schooner. A grey-bearded gentleman is busy readying the boat. Trying to sound like a sailor, I say "no wind", he answers, "Actually, it is perfect for sailing."

I begin asking more questions, and he finally replies, "Who are you?" implying, a reporter. Telling him about my earlier phone call to him, he breaks into a big smile (not always the reception I get). He adds, "Yes, I am Capt. Joe, of the *Capt. Kidd*. So glad to meet you." Soon he commences welcoming and processing couples, a family of women, and a photographer. A young woman smelling of competence boards and stores cameras and drinks. "Name is Nadine Perez, the deck hand," she informs me. Seems like a first mate to me.

Last spring Nadine was a passenger, watching another woman serve as the deck hand. A musician who plays the tuba and former motorcycle repairperson, Nadine had just moved to the Gulf Coast. She wanted to sail so Capt. Joe gave her a chance. She now ties knots, shoves off, sets and stores sails like a pro.

Come to find out women alumnus of Captain Joe include the J-class sailing coach at the Naval Academy and other instructional sailors. This outwardly gruff old sailor clearly has a soft spot for mentoring young sailors. A retired chemical worker, Joe Stumpf and his wife, Cathy, turned a hobby into two businesses, Capt. Kidd and the Tropical Express gift shop.

Setting sail, "Aaargh, maties," booms out as Capt. Kidd provides an interesting safety briefing including how to use the head (you don't just flush). With sails set, Capt. Joe sighs relaxing at the wheel, just as we do returning across the causeway. Looks like you are on vacation, I observe. Nodding yes, he launches into sailing stories, crossing the Gulf seven times, DR, dead reckoning, Belize, close calls, music and friendships. Plus, the trials of building the boat, while meeting strict Coast Guard certifications. Licensed for up to 28 guests, it is the only one in the area.

The photographer is a young man, Arthur, a seasoned deep-sea diver who trains astronauts at NASA. Nadine, with her modified Mohawk hairdo, and musical notes tattooed on the side of her head creates imagines of Tommy McGee and Janis Joplin. Perfect for sailing. The quiet sea slips by, the Texas size sun sets and Caribbean musical sounds of Kelly McGuire hypnotize us as we traverse the Bay.

Thanks, Capt. Joe and Nadine, for doing more than staring at the sea.

A Mountain Sailing Story

Driving through the east side of the Sandia (watermelon) Mountains brings back many memories for me. The first was at 6 years old on our way to ski at La Madera, then a rope tow slope. Today it is the world's longest tramway, rising from the west side of the mountain, on the edge of Albuquerque. As wonderful as the flight up the Tram is, I still prefer the drive. Turning off the Turquoise Trail, the back way to Santa Fe, we stop at the Tinkertown Museum. Talk about memories, it was probably 1984 the last time I was here with our kids. Begun in 1962, by Ross (R.J.) Ward, this very unique, only-in-New-Mexico work of largely one family, opened to the public in 1983. Entering through glass bottle walls and a maze of funky wooden halls is a kids-of-all-ages collection of dioramas, one-person band juke box, carvings, sayings, dolls and a full size ocean-going boat.

A boat in the mountains? Not in my memory. Heading straight for the gift shop and hopefully a helpful docent, I ask the owner. "How and when did the boat get here?"

"It was my brother's, and 1994," she replies.

"Oh, so it's new." Truth is, I am older.

Better informed, I rush back to the boatshed for further study. The *Theodora R* (*TR*), built in 1936, is still a proud sturdy 35-foot single mast sailboat. The story goes *TR* did not take kindly to being brought to the mountains. Today three youngsters from San Antonio gently touch the teak deck, the bowsprit, and examine the huge wall map tracing *TR* travels on a ten-year trip around the world. Awe of the accomplishment appears as each new family realizes the treasure before us. *TR* appears content.

Not expecting a wharf story today, I find the owner busy answering questions and running the shop. Soon asking my own questions, she suggests purchasing a couple of books, *Ten Years Behind the Mast* and *Plunge,* (available on Amazon) both by Fritz Damler. They are a bargain and my binge reading begins.

The next day, having finished *Ten Years,* I am back, asking the owner if she is Carla, Fritz's sister. Yes, and R. J.'s widow. She suggests reading the award-winning *Plunge* for the rest of the story.

Fritz and Mari on their beach on Crooked Island

Travel and Tolerance: Fritz Damler

Painted on a plank at Tinkertown, New Mexico, is a famous statement. "Travel is fatal to prejudice, bigotry, and narrow-mindedness, and many of our people need it sorely on these accounts. Broad, wholesome, charitable views of men and things cannot be acquired by vegetating in one little corner of the Earth all one's lifetime." Mark Twain (1869).

After reading the quote I am staring at the sailboat, *Theodora R* (TR), from every angle, stretching my imagination to ten years aboard this small boat, exploring the world. Beginning life in England in 1936, *TR* now lives under a boat shed in the mountains of New Mexico.

The man who partnered with *TR* on this cruise, Fritz Damler, now resides on a Crooked Island, Bahamas, beach. He used to live next door to the boat shed way before *TR* arrived. How this mountain-dwelling man came to live next to the water and TR, the sailboat in New Mexico, would make a wonderful film. It's all in his book, *Ten Years Behind the Mast* (Amazon).

Fritz must be the most tolerant person in the world. Come to find out, he is very easy-going, self-sufficient and adaptable. Circumnavigating the world with *TR* (and no GPS) he met many of the most interesting and exasperating people, and that's just his family. Only kidding, his sister, Carla, and his mother met him every so often, from New Zealand to Puerto Rico. Crewmembers paid ten dollars a day for the adventure, which included fresh seafood. Sign me on.

And adventure they got, wave by wave as Fritz says, 100-foot waves, not to mention, sharks, reefs, pirates, boat repairs and idyllic days with friends. During a full decade at sea, he experienced it all: discovery, heartbreak, misadventure and as all Galvestonians can relate, saltwater.

After building guitars, selling Turkish rugs and writing books, Fritz settled on the southern tip of the Bahamas for home. His "retirement" included building his beach house from the sand up, encountering mosquitos and making new friends. And also, with Mari, writing *Plunge* (Amazon), a wonderful chronicle of this venture. Written from a "he said, she felt", view, or Mars and Venus go to remote Bahamian island, you understand the need for a charitable view of others.

With only one pay phone on the island, Fritz and Mari thankfully can somehow email me. He did not stay in his one corner of the earth. This is a man who took the plunge into a very exciting and rewarding life. Imagine what Mark Twain would say.

Living the Dream Aboard a Large Power Motor Boat

Turning 51, Kristan Rojas realized she didn't know what she wanted from life. As a wife, mother and granddaughter, she had always done what others wanted. Single, with adult children doing fine, it was her turn. While most live-aboard dreams begin on the sofa, Rojas first examined recreational vehicles as she put her Conroe home on the market.

Rojas, a Houston native, was drawn to the water. Limited RV spaces on Galveston beaches generated a search for boats.

Mark Nicholas, author of *The Essentials of Living Aboard a Boat*, on his YouTube video sums it up: "Liveaboarders sip margaritas, listening to Jimmy Buffet, while discussing sewage, electrode and girl problems. This lifestyle must come from within the person."

Contacting Tommy Tipton of Lauderdale Yacht Sales in South Shore Harbour, Rojas found *Ocean Chase.* While the boat was well worn, Rojas fell for it.

"This boat transaction was far from typical," Tipton said.

Tipton realized Rojas was the exception to the rule; first boat owners should avoid fixer-uppers. "With her record of flipping houses she was realistic."

The owner met Rojas and soon realized she could be *Ocean's* savior. After a survey found that the boat had excellent bones and engines but cosmetically was a moldy mess, the owner greatly reduced the price.

The James Krogen designed power cruiser, built in 1969, originally sold for $600,000, far more than Rojas paid. The boat is 54 feet long, has a beam of 17 feet and draws less than four feet. Powered by two 425-HP diesel engines, it can cruise at 11 knots. As a generous live-aboard, it comes with three berths and two heads. Only four were built. Rojas is searching for the others.

Liveaboards offer freedom. You can choose where you live and who your neighbors are. And the constant gentle motion can remove cobwebs from your head.

The Galveston Yacht Basin proved to be the perfect dock to heal the *Ocean Chase*. Scrubbing, sealing and cleaning for seven months full-time brought it back shipshape

Becoming a bit stir crazy, Rojas considered ways to get off the boat and make a bit of cash. Hooks Bar and Grill just opened on the lower Strand, so Rojas was off to bartending—adult day care, as she calls it. Her PT convertible can be found out front five days a week. Occasionally on weekends, Rojas motors *Ocean* out of the basin.

While the boat does not require a captain's license, she is more comfortable offshore with Capt. Blake Eubanks at the controls. "She is an adventurous, energetic and determined lady," Eubanks adds.

Rojas's dream is to scale-up seasideshop.biz, her online business, and to take short cruises, perhaps expanding to charters in the next year or two.

"I believe people who choose the live-aboard lifestyle definitely fit a unique personality profile, and Kristan has it," Eubanks said.

Living Right Onboard a 32-Foot Sailboat

Adelante, moving forward, is not only the name of Roan Wright's 32-foot, it describes his lifestyle. Tied to the last pier in Clear Lake's Legends Pointe Marina, the boat has everything Zoe, his big brown-eyed canine companion, and he need. Zoe, a year-old rescue dog, mostly terrier, has her bed on a counter in the galley just down the entrance ladder.

The main cabin, confidential closet size, has wood walls with built in furniture. Forward is a small bunkroom. Wright's motto is go small, go now. Yet, for a man and his dog, there is space, everything in its place. A crockpot, sink, icebox and freezer, with storage snuck in everywhere, complete the galley. "There just isn't room to entertain on this style of boat," Wright said.

Wright's life on a sailboat began with his father's itchy feet. His dad worked in shipping traffic-management at ports, so they moved around Texas. His mom's family homesteaded in Possum Walk, north of Houston.

Growing up around water afforded Wright the opportunity to learn to sail. In a Lightning 19 sailboat he often navigated Lake Conroe and Travis.

After graduating from commercial art school, Wright joined his dad, by then a sports editor, in Caracas, Venezuela and later in Barcelona, Spain. Wright taught English and proofread for a newspaper. He migrated into printing, which had been his occupation since 1992.

Wright returned to Houston to care for his parents. After they died, Wright was melancholy, staying home, slowly sorting for three years until he had everything in a five-by-ten-foot storage shed. Untethered, he could move forward. "Living on a sailboat seemed to be the right thing for me," Wright said.

Wright sails almost every weekend, only not on his boat. "It takes a good three hours just to secure everything before I can sail," he said. Off-shore sailing is inspiring for Wright. He likes the thrill of being on the sea out of sight of land.

Aboard his boat Wright enjoys the gentle rocking rhythm of his life. He eats out often. It feeds his social life too. "I've made some wonderful friends at my drinking and eating establishments around South Shore. We all have a lot in common," Wright said.

Day to day life exists maintaining the boat. "You can do as much or as little maintenance as you want on a sailboat, depending on how you use it," he said. Everyday sailing requires tight unworn lines, good sails and a smooth-running engine.

On the other hand, a semi-permanent docked live aboard is less upkeep and thus less sailing. "I have a bow sprit that needs to be replaced and an engine tune-up before I take this boat out sailing again," Wright said. While comfortable, Wright is not looking to stay put forever. He purchased a Bruce Roberts

Seamaster, a 45-foot project boat, in Georgia. "It's large enough to entertain on," Wright said. "Florida might be a good place to explore," he mused, stroking his beard.

Seizing the Spring Seas: Tall Ships to Cruise Liners

The boat's white bow sprit kept heading up, rising slowly into the clouds as I braced myself with the wheel. The bow paused and traced back down almost into the green white crowned waves. The *Gazelle's* rudder didn't respond until well after the process began again. "Keep it on 60 degrees," the strong voice of Capt. Loren Cadenhead echoed. Easy for him to say as we crested each wave the sailboat yawed and the compass went from 50° back to 70°. I thought, "That averages 60, right?"

We were out watching the tall ship parade off the beautiful Galveston Beaches. Running parallel to the *When and If*, Gen. Patton's schooner. It was if we had sailed back to the 1800s. Google Tall Ships Galveston for more history and photos.

Clouds of sails emerged on the horizon quickly closing to where we could make out human figures like ants scrambling up the nets on the *Picton Castle*. We were having the time of our lives at almost a 45-degree angle, spray flying.

Cozumel three days later. As I yelled "Coming about," Capt. Tom instructed, "Head for the cruise ship." We were flying, one twitch of the wheel set the bow off course. The Canadian *True North IV*, was the 12-metre sailboat of the 1987 America's Cup. A jet compared to the Sea Star Base *Gazelle*.

On each boat the new crew bonded rapidly, though they had different perspectives. *Gazelle*, mostly older folks with years of sailing experience, where I was the newbie. A Naval sailor on USS *Midway*, a Wall Street broker, realtor and an ocean racer—and that's just Byron and Sallie. I was the novice.

The Canadian boat crew were all young tourists and first-time sailors. I became the old salt, a veteran of seven races—only one loss.

The *Gazelle* crew will become friends for years, the 12-metre crew never to be seen again. Yet on the sea, the crews, one vessel, five knots in six-foot chop, the other sleek and fast, were all in the same boat—all pulling together. A broader lesson to be applied to our nation?

Thanks to Sea Star Base Galveston's Community Sailing, Texas A&M-Galveston, and the Galveston Historic Foundation, especially Mark Scibinico for permitting us to relive history and etch new memories. And thanks to the *True North IV* crew for winning. The week was a jack pot for me: tall ships, a 12-metre boat and a cruise ship home, including a perfect view of USS *Stewart* and *Cavalla* at sunrise. A wonderful way to seize the spring seas and forge long-term and instant relationships with memories. And Galveston is right in the middle of it all. Can't wait till summer. Oh, wait what was the temp today?

Sailplane Soaring in Retirement

Whoa! What did I get myself into now? I pull the yellow knob on the dash and the towline drops away. The small plane ahead of us peels off to the left. We drop to the right and my stomach goes queasy while my knees go weak. The story of how I am crammed into the cockpit of a sailplane at 10,000 feet while heading for a very dark thunderhead cloud goes way back.

It begins with my father obtaining his pilot's license at age fourteen. At seventeen, he joined the Navy during WWII to become a pilot. The Navy sent him to Columbia University, Princeton, and back to the University of New Mexico as the war ended. Dad always flew small planes. So, I grew up flying with him all over the west. I was never afraid and my stomach was always where it belonged, even bouncing around on hot summer days.

Later in life, Dad became a colonel in the Civil Air Patrol. In fact, he died in his flight suit minutes after completing a mission. The Lloyd A. Sallee Soaring Academy is named for him.

Last Christmas I received a Groupon for a high-performance sailplane flight. One requirement was you could not weigh over 240 lbs. Right out of the shower at UTMB, I weighed 240 lbs. Given that they probably wanted me dressed, my flight was at least five pounds in the future. Now at 198 pounds (plus shorts and t-shirt) I was ready to soar.

Groupon in hand I traveled to Moriarty, New Mexico, home of the USA Soaring Museum and where my dad gave soaring lessons. It is a great place to soar. Our family lore is that all of my brothers flew sailplanes with my dad. But I never had.

Author squeezed into glider ready to go

I found out Stan, my "instructor", had flown with my dad for many years and considered Dad "a prince of a man." At almost 6'4" (thanks to Pilates) I put the sailplane on like a tight pair of pants. We sailed over to the Sandia Mountains where my father's ashes are spread.

Soaring is the opposite of flying a plane. First, there is no engine. You need thermals which require jumping from the bottom of one cloud to the next like a huge roller coaster.

Second, you turn the stick right, and the nose goes left. A lot of rudder (at your feet) is needed to turn. Third, you fly by instruments and the seat of your pants. You must really focus—no daydreaming! And fourth, as Stan said, even seasoned aircraft pilots have trouble learning to soar. I sure understood.

Our (Stan's), landing was very smooth and fast as the ground is about three inches under my rear end. As we rolled to our parking space, I had learned another lesson from my dad, even though he is no longer with us.

Later that day when I called my brothers, I discovered that only one of them had ever soared with Dad. My brothers thought I was nuts. My stomach and knees agreed. My "sailing" will be in a boat on a smooth sea from now on.

What's in A Boat Name?

As most readers of this book now know, I really get into exploring boats and ships. From aircraft carriers, such as USS *Midway* in San Diego, to cruise ships, to bulk carriers and even 1936 sailboats now on display in the mountains of New Mexico. I'm intrigued by the history, construction, operation, and names of each craft.

Where the names of streets, cars and buildings came from interests me, too. When my 93-year-old mother was recognized by the University of New Mexico for an award last year, the MC said, "Not only does Mrs. Carol Sallee know the names of the buildings on our campus, she actually knew the people." True, she helped me know those folks through her stories.

Last week I visited with my friend, Fritz Damler, at Tinkertown in New Mexico. His boat *Theodora (TR)* which he sailed for 10 years around the world, is displayed here.

Tourists from New Jersey stopped, amazed how small *TR* is. They asked Fritz to take their photo, not realizing who he was. I stepped forward, made introductions, put Fritz with family and took the picture. My guess is that memories were made for this family, just by knowing Fritz's name.

So, what's in a name? Of course, in William Shakespeare's *Romeo and Juliet*, Juliet bemoaned the fact that Romeo's last name barred their love. Shakespeare wrote, "What's in a name? That which we call a rose, by any other name would smell as sweet." Wikipedia states, "The reference is often used to imply that the names of things do not affect what they really are."

So, is that true for boat names too? Can you change a boat's name? Legend has it, that is bad luck. Fritz Damler's *Thelma and the Whore of Babylon* (Amazon) is a tale of changing the name.

In the 1700s, Caribbean pirates were particularly superstitious so the British Navy spread the rumor that it was bad luck to change ship's names so they could track them.

At a garage sale, I picked up a book, *Let's Name It: 10,000 Boat Names for all Types of Watercraft*, by John Corcoran and Lew Hackler. They provide names listed by categories. From *All the World is a Stage* and *Bon Voyage* to *Smooth, Slick, and Saucy* and *Witches Brew*, the book explores why would anyone choose a name like that?

I still don't know, but plan to find out. After all, Texas A&M at Galveston's training ship, *General Rudder*, (see Chapter 9) lead me to learn about a great Texas A&M President.

Chapter 9 - World War II & Seawolf Park

Veteran WWII Stories Still Alive & Well at Seawolf Park

Driving over the bridge to Pelican Island, past A&M toward Seawolf Park, struck by the timeless draw of the sea. I am on my way to meet a busload of Brookdale senior citizens from Sugar Land. They include at least three WWII Veterans. A Navy nurse, radar/radio instructor and a destroyer escort (DE) officer.

While I had other things to do this morning—after all I am retired—I am not missing this opportunity. We are losing thousands of the greatest generation, and their significant stories.

Exiting the bus at the America Undersea Warfare Center, each 80-year-old or 90-something senior looks around the submarine, USS *Cavalla*, and the (DE) USS *Stewart* with an expression of puzzlement and awe. One self-assured gentleman comes down the stairs. I ask,"Dick Hoffman?"

"Yes, sir," he replies. Full of energy, in command, he begins the tour by telling the group about my columns. It is difficult to accept this group's thanks. We owe them so much.

A 19-year-old college student when WWII began, following graduation in 1943, Dick was commissioned as an ensign. He was assigned the essential role as the anti-submarine weapons officer on USS *Damon M. Cummings* (DE) 643. For fifteen-months straight, the *Cummings* stayed in the far Pacific. Tenders came to them, thus no liberty. A hospital ship came into view once and every gun trained on it. Dick was alarmed until he realized each gun had a telescope and the hospital ship had nurses.

After escorting half of a 1,000-ship armada to Okinawa, his ship shot down a Kamikaze. They served picket duty so close to Okinawa the battle looked like a movie through binoculars. April 18th, word spread through the ship that popular folksy frontline columnist Ernie Pyle had been killed onshore by a sniper. Even though they were very used to bad news—four destroyers damaged or sunk one afternoon by Kamikazes—with Pyle's death, sadness fell across the ship. As Dick told me this story, my stomach took a blow.

I knew Ernie Pyle, though not personally—he died before I was born. As a kindergartner, the first library I visited was his Albuquerque home. Just last summer I returned after re-reading one of his books. The small house with white picket fence is the same as when he left in 1944.

Small things change our lives. A Japanese bullet wounded a Marine. Sent home early, he wooed and married Dick's girl. Not yet eligible for discharge and promoted to executive officer, Dick and the *Cummings* went to China. Two years and a law degree later, Dick met his wife-to-be, married her and enjoyed a boundless family life. When his wife passed, he was eighty-two and lost.

A friend suggested that Dick volunteer on USS *Stewart*. He began by scraping rust on the deck. Over his tenure he helped rewrite by-laws, obtained historic designation for the *Stewart*, and chaired several committees. At ninety-three, as emeritus board member and veteran, Dick Hoffman in still serving.

CPO on USS *Stewart*

Expecting a "greatest generation" WWII-era sailor, disappointment seeps into my thoughts as I sit down. Chief Petty Officer Mac Christy appears to be a few years younger than me. At least the drive to Seawolf Park was nice on this bright winter day.

The stern of *Stewart* has a watertight door at ground level—clearly something new. Knocking on the door, Dewayne Davis welcomed me into a ship wide dining room with hanging bunks ceiling to floor forward.

As often, my first impression is wrong. CPO Christy joined the Navy in 1951, when I was a year old. He has a 20-year-old's twinkle in his eye and enthusiasm to match. The next few hours are filled with details of life aboard a destroyer escort, such as USS *Stewart* (DE-238)—untold battles, interpersonal dynamics, and complex large machines.

CPO Christy is past chairman of the board of the Cavalla Historical Foundation, responsible for the vessels in the American Undersea Warfare Center. He is also president of the Edsall Class Veterans Association. He's in Galveston four times a year for meetings and workweeks.

Restoration and preservation began on the *Stewart* upon its arrival in 1973. During its long and distinguished service (see Wikipedia), this football field-long ship was the home to 189 sailors and eight officers. In later service, changes in equipment reduced the number of crew. During dangerous cruises, a sailor's life aboard the *Stewart* included tight sleeping quarters, primitive open restrooms, small offices, mess hall and galley. The war room, and even the captain's cabin, were cramped.

Launched in 1942, the *Stewart* still looks pretty good, thanks to a dedicated, diverse group of volunteers. They scrape, paint, fix and repair, and include phone linemen, MIT scientists, cooks, air traffic controllers, and hardware store clerks. All lend their expertise and elbow grease to make the ship whole. They create a living history for our computerized youth, allowing them to feel, smell and witness the sacrifices sailors made and still make today.

As we begin our tour, CPO Christy greets two 20-something young men as they debark. "Any questions?" he asks. "Yes, about the engines ..." Fifteen minutes later after a detailed discussion of the diesel engines (none of which I understood), the young men agree to come to workweek.

Who would have thought these young men knew so much about WWII engines? CPO Christy did and made the 60-year connection. You don't get that from a book but rather from years of teaching young men how to become sailors. Come to find out, the young men are engineers on diesel tugs. E-mail machief@hughes.net to join Chief Christy for a workweek.

CPO Mac Christy USN (Ret.) and USS Stewart

USS Stewart stands proudly, still serving

On the Rack Aboard USS *Stewart*

Dad would never believe what I am doing this week. It all began on The Strand when Dewayne drove by in a pickup with the American Undersea Warfare Center decals on it. Picking up my clam cell phone I call the number. "Hi, I am driving right behind you and would like to write a column." The call lead to meeting Chief Petty Officer (USN Retired) Mac Christy.

The Chief stayed in touch, inviting me to attend spring workweek. Signing up, I explained I would be at least an hour late, due to a doctor'sappointment. AWOL right off—yet never seeing a brig on the *Stewart*, I felt safe, until Chief Mac emailed that there was a spud locker that could serve as a jail.

Thanks to tornado warnings, the appointment was rescheduled so I was on time. Prior to workweek, I chose salvaging items off USS *Sturgis* to be used on the *Stewart* as my task. As the week began there was no *Sturgis* in sight, so I asked for another assignment.

Chief Mac asked, "Want to help Bill organize tools?"

"Sure," I replied.

Approaching this experience as a participant-observer-researcher, I seriously doubted I'd be accepted as part of the group, but something special happened. By dinnertime, we resembled long-time shipmates.

What a diverse bunch of guys and gals (1940's-speak, when the *Stewart* was built). F-15 pilots, air traffic controllers telling them where to go, antique-store owners, mechanics, scientists, nurses, U.S. Army, Air Force, Coast Guard and Navy members, young, old and none of the above.

Micro, Mezzo and Macro social systems dynamics are topics in some of my books. For sure this group does not fit the normal. A new area for research? Well it isn't going to be me doing it; I am retired and having fun.

Shipmates, friends and wander-ins—all are welcomed and set to work under the gentle guidance of Chief Mac. Later I am assigned painting the container roof with some stuff that costs $1,000.

Thankfully, Jerry, a professional painter, shows up at the last minute, saying he had read about workweek in the paper. I became his assistant real quick!

As kids, we watched 8mm movies, taken by Dad, of depth charges being dropped off the rack on a destroyer's stern—exploding in huge domes of water. My submariner uncles did not find the film as interesting. Working with Dave, from Boerne, I am priming the racks from which the charges were rolled. Not sure Dad, as an officer, ever knew all the nooks this rack possesses! Dad did value being a shipmate. After this experience, I have a hint of that, too. What a crew! And there is no spud locker. Chief Mac is just very keen at group dynamics. Email machief@hughes.net.

Chief Biro USS *Stewart* Plank-Owner

Hanging over the front of the pulpit, I stretched far over. No, it was not Sunday, and, no, I was not in church preaching. I was on USS *Stewart's* top deck, fifty feet up in a lookout platform painting the antenna platform below.

This was a special day. Chief Rudy Biro, a plank owner and original crewmember, was coming back aboard. He was traveling all the way from Maryland, just as he did in 1943, this time with his family.

Soon I heard a yell, "The chief's here." Scrambling down, I joined Chief Biro on the second deck, up where almost exactly 75 years ago he manned his station as a gunnery chief. I gladly sat down on hard steel to visit. This time he was in a lawn chair—no sitting when he served.

Beginning at the beginning, he said he was born by the Naval Shipyard in D.C.

I exclaimed, "Oh, you were born in Anacostia."

He looked at me with renewed interest. "Yes, I was."

"When I was a baby, my family lived there while Dad was at sea," I replied.

Rudy joined the naval reserves while in high school for the summer cruises and monthly stipend. He was called to active duty a year before Pearl Harbor was attacked.

Aboard USS *George F. Elliott*, a transport ship, Rudy fell three decks when a board broke. After being in a coma with broken bones for thirty days he joined USS *Hamul*, a destroyer-escort tender. Meanwhile, USS *Elliott* was sunk. Arriving too early in Galveston to join USS *Stewart*, still in dry dock, Chief Biro did guard duty.

Heroic adventures soon followed. USS *Stewart*, with USS *Edsall*, saved a burning oil tanker and rescued survivors, earning national recognition. During D-Day, the June 6, 1944 invasion to retake Europe from the Nazis, Chief Biro aboard USS *Stewart*, sailed just out of the English Channel in the Atlantic, protecting the flank of the largest fleet in history from German U-boats.

Chief Biro's family believed he shared a cabin, but as a chief (I learned from Chief Mac during several workweeks), he bunked in the "goat-locker" forward. This area is being restored and is not open to the public.

With solemn promises to be careful, Chief Biro's adult kids went down one level to the goat-locker where twelve chiefs slept, ate and hung out. The stainless-steel refrigerator, restored by Texas A&M-Galveston cadets, is still there. Forward were the heads. Daughter-in-law Mary videoed, while son, Rich, asked me questions.

Topside, the video brought a deep, memory-lit smile to the Chief's eyes. Just that smile made all the work of volunteers from all over the county worth it. A small reward for a remarkable man and those who gave so much.

Chief Biro continued to serve for 26 years as a D.C. police lieutenant. He went on to work with his best buddy from service aboard USS *Stewart*, Richard Paugh, a manager at NCR Corporation.

With Spencer, another volunteer, we climbed down with Chief Biro's walker. Chief Biro descended the ladders of his youth one more time, still a strong, self-assured and independent man of the sea.

History Comes Alive on Galveston's USS *Stewart*

Sitting across from me in USS *Stewart's* volunteer's mess deck are two young women. One portrays a WAVE and the other a Red Cross Volunteer. Their uniforms, hairdos, down to their shoes and purses are all from WWII, just like the ship.

My pen flies trying to keep up with the moving details they share of the life of WWII women in uniform on the front lines, far from relatives and comforts of home.

Leslie Lee, of Dallas, explains that people often think she is a nurse in her uniform, yet she is portraying a Red Cross volunteer. Her role was to educate and visit, in this case, sailors. She would teach sailors how to dance while talking to them.

Dancing is apropos for Leslie. For 16 years she has attended hanger dances. What is a hanger dance? You wear what you have in your closet on hangers? She replies with a polite laugh, "No, it is an airplane hangar dance." She visits vintage stores in person and online looking for authentic uniforms for the dances. The dances are to swing music. While Bob Wills is still the king, the music is by Glenn Miller and the Andrews Sisters.

Dances were used to help with emotional issues sailors might face. Wholesome female recruits reminded sailors of why they were fighting, that people still cared, and what was going to be there when the war was over.

As Gen. Dwight Eisenhower stated in his address to the U.S. Congress June 18, 1945, "The Red Cross, with its clubs for recreation, its coffee and doughnuts in the forward areas, its readiness to meet the needs of the well and to help minister to the wounded ... has often seemed to be the friendly hand of this nation reaching across the sea to sustain its fighting men."

The Red Cross Congressional charter clarified the role as, "furnish volunteer aid to the sick and wounded of armies in time of war." Leslie brought this to life, right in front of us.

Sara Boswell of Austin is wearing a WAVES seersucker uniform. She explains that WAVES—Women Accepted for Volunteer Emergency Service (I think they wanted the acronym)—became a branch of the US Naval Reserve in 1942.

WAVES, officers, and enlisted women began in office support and administrative roles as yeomen. The number increased to over 86,000 with only seventy-two women of color. The roles of WAVES expanded to include engineers, mechanics, hospital corpsmen, air traffic controllers and radio operators.

Sara describes how the Japanese captured three enlisted WAVES on Bataan in the early days of WWII. The Japanese didn't know what to do with the women, who gave their rank as officers. During the terrible internment, the WAVES kept track of the diets and monitored caloric intake, helping to keep even 90 lb. soldiers alive. The American Dietary Association employed the WAVES' records after the war. We learned so much—history, fashion—from this reenactment.

Sara Boswell of Austin in WWII Red Cross uniform

Rust Never Sleeps, but You Can Aboard USS *Stewart*

Maybe rust never sleeps aboard USS *Stewart* (DE-238) but you can during the November workweek. Bunks are waiting for the first thirty "sailors" who sign up. For the week, you will eat better and more than even on a cruise ship. All tax deductible, too. And no one gets seasick either—guaranteed.

A diverse crew, ages ten to eighty-two, join to scrape, grind, prime and paint over rust. As all Galvestonians know, rust attacks relentlessly and everywhere. My bike spokes only lasted six months in the garage, now the bike is back in the house.

The *Stewart* sits proudly next to submarine *Cavalla* in the American Undersea Warfare Center in Seawolf Park, bows pointed out to sea. On this small peninsula, it's surrounded by sea-salt water, rust fuel carried on the breeze. First sight for arriving ships and the last view for departing cruise line passengers, the *Stewart* and *Cavalla* are landmarks for sure. As Capt. Vandy Anderson, who helped obtain the *Stewart*, tells the inland folks, "the *Stewart* is the gray one."

Actually, it is haze gray. Thousands of gallons brighten its sides, bent from waves of days gone by. Volunteers work hard all year to maintain the 1942 ship. It has come a long way over the past five years, with most of the public areas now fully restored.

Known as a small destroyer, the escorts protected the slow-moving convoys of Liberty and Victory ships during WWII, which supplied forces on land with everything from napkins to bombs. The slowest ship set the pace often traveling no more than ten mph. The escorts, like the *Stewart*, were fast enough to move in and out of formation and chase German U-boat submarines on the surface.

Volunteers come and go as their schedule allows over the week. Arrive at 7 a.m. and your cooked-to-order omelet awaits you, with fruit, rolls, strong coffee, homemade everything. Mike cooks, Susan bakes, I am told. Not sure what that means other than you will never eat such enjoyable food, or so much! Lunch and dinner, not to mention desserts, are out of this world. Mike explains the food is not free—you work for it, and you do. A noble set of sore muscles each night. A worthy job, sound sleep.

Working on the Stewart you learn the ship's details. Amazing how fast it was built in the Texas Brown Shipyard. You sense how the crew worked (there are no chairs on the decks) and lived. The smell of diesel, paint and sweat comes free with the experience, too. Today thousands of men and women are aboard the modern versions of USS *Stewart*, still protecting our interests around thc world. Most of us are younger than the *Stewart*, though not always looking as good. Each workweek, volunteer labor beats back the rust, revealing the true *Stewart* and *Cavalla*, living wonders. A DE and submarine that provided us the freedom to disagree and still work together on a common vision. To join us:
www.americanunderseawarfare.org or machief@hughes.net.

USS Cavalla battle flag with ships sunk

Two Girls and A Submarine

Following two young women up the stairs, we walk at a slower rate onto the deck of a WWII submarine, USS *Cavalla*. Jordan, a 10-year-old, is giving a tour to Nicole, our 8-year-old granddaughter. Jordan's dad, DeWayne Davis, is the American Undersea Warfare Center curator. Leaning over to him, I whisper, "This should be interesting."

Glancing down through the deck slats, we see the pressurized hull, a twenty-seven-foot pipe strengthened for 300-foot depths. The outer structure includes ballast and fuel tanks, a sharp bow and large superstructure, and the thirty-foot high sail, which Tony just finished welding and painting. It is a beautiful deep black that sets off a large white 244, *Cavalla's* place in the line of submarines and in history.

Following the girls, I duck down the stairs to the forward torpedo room through the original loading hatch. Ducking—an action and word I cannot use enough for anyone six feet or taller—we enter another world of sights and smells. Torpedoes line the walls with bunks between them, mattresses wrapped in heavy plastic, not for hygiene but to prevent fire.

Contorting myself through the first watertight "doorway" I hear the girls in a very serious discussion. No giggling or "normal" preadolescent behavior, it is as if a spell has been cast. Most tourists exploring the boat become quiet, reverent and serious, too.

Entering officers' quarters, without doors, Jordan explains, are the small galley and mess table. Shuffling a bit aft to the ship's office, which is smaller than a phone booth (do kids today even know what that is?), there is a typewriter. Do kids ...? Never mind. Moving on to the crew's mess hall next to an RV-sized kitchen, is the galley where two cooks feed eighty-nine men.

Still ducking, into the control room, we squeeze up a narrow ladder, normally closed, to the conning tower, a 6 X 12-foot cramped space, where twelve sailors established targets on a computer consisting of dials. Do kids today—? Now they do. Lining up a shot through the periscope from the place the Japanese aircraft carrier was sunk makes this very real. Moved, I stand down.

The girls quickly move through the battery and engine rooms as I struggle to get 210 pounds through another watertight doorframe. Reaching the end of our football-field-long tour we emerge from the aft torpedo room.

Kids today race through everything. I wonder if Nicole absorbed the guts, skill and knowledge it took to operate this complex machine. My question is soon answered. Her dad and 3-year-old sister, the Ball High mascot namesake, Tornado, arrive for their tour.

Nicole insists she conduct the tour, not Grandpa. Before reaching the first hatch, I am chastised for interfering with her presentation. Point made. In great detail, she tells the submarine and its crew's story. Okay her generation will do just fine, even if they don't know what a phone booth is. Check out the YouTube: How a WWII submarine works.

Tony Can Fix It

It is an early spring day in Seawolf Park on Pelican Island. The park includes the American Undersea Warfare Center with spectacular views in every direction. Across the bay is Bolivar Lighthouse, ferries rushing past every few minutes. This is the junction for five ship channels, a huge intersection with no stoplights.

On the point is one ship, Destroyer Escort USS *Stewart* and one boat, a submarine, USS *Cavalla*, bows pointing out to sea. Next to the *Cavalla* is a stack of 2x4 foot wood boards. Great, I think, something I know about, lumber. (Not sure how wood works on steel ships.) I ask Tony Martinez, the welder par excellent. He is going to build a scaffold on the narrow deck next to the submarine's sail. The sail is often mistakenly called the conning tower. The large thirty-foot tall structure has rust in several places, which require new plates.

Offering my help building the scaffolding, Tony quietly declines even after I list my construction credentials. I guess I would want to build the contraption I'd be standing on sixty feet off the ground, too. He agrees to let me bring the lumber up on the sub.

Over the next few months, through the hot, humid summer, I watch from far below in admiration of his expertise. Not only welding with art and skill, he makes steel replacements from scratch with no special tools. My repeated offers to help are politely declined.

One day I catch Tony doing "normal" work, painting upside down under one of the *Stewart's* gun tubs. Proudly stating I painted the other tub, he answers he knows. It looks good, he says. A door to this man just opened. He shares that he learned to weld on his family's 1,800-acre farm in Oklahoma. He watched a hired hand and then tried it, no lessons.

Moving to Galveston at the request of his wife—a good practice to follow—he hired on with the Parks Board about 20 years ago. One boss learned Tony could weld anything. Soon Tony was off the beach and into the shop. About 15 years ago he began welding the new deck plates on the *Cavalla*, the rest is little known history.

Arriving each afternoon at the center after working at the parks board, he goes straight to work. He shows me different types of welds, the seams of steel rippling between sheets of steel.

Seventy years ago, the Brown Shipyard of Orange, Texas worker's skills can still be found all over the *Stewart*. Painting different sections I am amazed at their welding proficiency. Tony shows me welding by others over the years. It is not as good. Poor welds leave small spots which collect water, and rust. He goes back to work. In my mind, I hear Chief Mac say, "That's no problem, Tony can fix it." And Tony always does, another unsung hero aboard these ships.

Tony's work on USS Cavalla underway

From Typo to Naval Captain

On a warm autumn day in 1935, battleships laid at anchor in the Long Beach Bay. A large flat-bottomed "Liberty" boat approached the wharf, spilling a hundred sailors out, landlubbers for a day. Five 10-year-old boys jumped on for the return trip to the ship. Boarding the USS *Pennsylvania*, the boys roamed the main deck, like kids do on the USS *Texas* today.

On the return ride, Wally, one of the boys, decided his life goal was to attend the Naval Academy and become an officer. At age fourteen, in the heart of the Depression, he learned the brutal truth. As the son of an enlisted sailor with no political connections, he hadn't a chance of attending the Academy.

Three years later Pearl Harbor was attacked. Entering at the lowest rank, Wally became a Navy signalman on Merchant

Marine ships. Four years and 14 trips across the Pacific later, he saw a notice announcing the V-12 program. This expansion of the Academy, through selected universities, would prepare 100,000 new officers. Wally was first in line for the exam.

Passing the exam opened a big bright door for Wally. Asked which university he wanted to attend, he said, "University of Washington." The instructor said, "Fine, UW it is." A few days later, his orders arrived. He was to report to Washburn College in Topeka, Kansas. The typist had made a typo.

Not discouraged, he packed for the heartland, far from the sea.

Completing his two semesters and playing on the football team, he was sent with all Washburn Navy grads to the next school. They boarded a train to the University of New Mexico (UNM), on the Rio Grande.

He excelled at UNM, too. Before long, he was announcing football on the radio, engaged to a wonderful girl and head of the Navy ROTC Midshipmen unit.

Leading the unit running of the track at 5:30 a.m. in July, 1945, half the sky instantly blasted light. No noise or wind, just bright light. It was the first A-bomb test, 130 miles south in the desert.

On graduation day, he led the midshipmen in parade, was best man at one wedding and groom at his own that evening. He attended to every detail, including tapping each bride with the broad side of a sword as she walked under the sword arch.

At 10 a.m. the next day, he and Suzy, his bride, headed out driving to San Francisco for his first assignment on a destroyer as an ensign. A Naval officer at last. Over the next decades he advanced to the rank of captain. Only one other person has risen from the lowest rank like Captain Wallace A. Greene did. Finishing his story last week, I said, "Uncle Wally, if it hadn't been for that typo, you wouldn't have married Aunt Suzy and we wouldn't be sitting here right now."

"Many small disappointments turned into good fortune in my career," he responded.

That is one typo that I am glad was made.

Just in Time at the Wharf

He arrived at the wharf just in time. No, he was not a late cruise ship passenger. This story begins with a childhood dream of becoming a Naval Officer. Ensign Wallace (Uncle Wally) A. Greene, was commissioned through the V-12 program during WWII. He entered as a Reserve Officer. Following WWII and three years aboard destroyers he wanted to be regular Navy.

The quickest path in 1949 was to get his dolphins, the pins awarded to qualified submarine officers. Soon, with Aunt Suzy, he was off to New London, Connecticut for sub school. Graduating, he was given orders to report to the USS *Remora* (487), in Japan. He had seven days to drive across the country before reporting in San Francisco.

He and Aunt Suzy set off at a leisurely pace. Every morning he dialed in CBS news. Four days into the trip, CBS announced the invasion of South Korea by the North. He drove straight to San Francisco. Walking into the Naval Personnel Office he stated his name. The personnel officer said, "We've been waiting for you, Mr. Greene. You're needed in Japan ASAP. Be at the bus stop in thirty minutes. You are going on the *Boxer*." He was a bit puzzled. Why was he wanted in Japan so quick, the Navy was putting him on an aircraft carrier, not a plane. Arriving at the dock an hour later, he rushes aboard as the lines were let loose. The carrier was packed with P-51 airplanes. Even the elevators had planes on them. Setting sail at thirty-two knots—most cruise ships go about twenty-two knots—the *Boxer* raced to Japan on the great circle course following the curve of the Earth. Theplanes were desperately needed in Korea.

With a record crossing, the *Boxer* pulled into Yokosuka, faster than flying island to the island. Wally and ten other submariners were the first ushered off. A Jeep and truck were waiting. The Jeep driver yelled, "Who's Greene? Get in." Off at breakneck speed, they pulled up to a submarine nest, where six subs were tied-up side to side.

The middle sub was getting underway. Uncle Wally saw a large 487 on the sail. He didn't need to be told to run. Boarding the *Remora*, the captain said, "You are junior officer of the watch." Wally was handed binoculars as he passed his sea bag to a sailor.

An hour later, clear of the harbor, the Captain ordered, "Mr. Greene, take us down to 280 feet." His first official dive. Eight other officers piled into the small control room (like the *Cavalla's*) to watch the new guy mess up. Thanks to a cold thermal layer, he was able to level off just right, even at two knots, much to the disappointment of his new fellow officers.

The captain was impressed with Uncle Wally. As was the Navy with his service, which later included command of the *Albacore*, the first sub with a curved bow.

Being early paid off, maybe that is where I got it.

Tolling the Boats

A stiff breeze blew the half-mast flags to attention. The sea, gray as the bow of USS *Stewart*, accented by the pitch-black hull of USS *Cavalla*. Standing behind a hundred seated former *Cavalla* sailors and officers, I witnessed the Tolling for the Boats ceremony at Seawolf Park.

Held during the *Cavalla* reunion for both boats the World War II *Cavalla*, on display here, and the nuclear version SSN 684, the ceremony began after 1945. Captain Gary Bell, a former ensign on the first *Cavalla*, and Chairman of the Cavalla Historical Foundation (CHF) welcomed the guests. ET1(SS) Don Goldsbury read the list of the 65 submarines with crews lost since 1900, most from 1943 to 1944 in the South Pacific. By percentage, it's the deadliest service in the U.S. military.

Commander Bryan Lethcoe, president (CHF), provided a portrayal of the last hours of USS *Seawolf*, accidentally sunk in 1944 by a USS destroyer escort similar to *Stewart*. In detail, Lethcoe described the loss of USS *Thresher* in 1963. I knew this story from another perspective, that of a nephew. The only information my family had was that a sub out of Portsmouth beginning with a "T" had sunk. Uncle Wally's boat was the *Tirante* and I felt the emotion of loss. But only for a day, as we learned of the loss for other families.

Over 4,000 young men have lost their lives serving in the

United States submarine force. The tolling of the bell, two rings for each submarine on eternal patrol, reminded us the debt of gratitude we owe to departed shipmates, as well as those still on active duty.

A wreath was laid upon the sea by two ladies representing families who look out to sea for the return of their loved ones.

The memorial service reaffirmed to Navy submarine personnel that deeds and sacrifices followed in the steps of those who preceded them. Their accomplishments did not come easy or without the "can do" spirit of those who wear the Dolphin insignia with pride and dignity.

Only here in Galveston is the full story of the American undersea warfare experienced, only here is a submarine next to the ship designed to sink submarines.

Over four hundred fourth graders and their teachers toured the boat and ship the two days before the ceremony. Next up is workweek. To restore, preserve and educate is the foundation's mission. And yes, mission accomplished.

Memorial Day Brought to Life at Seawolf Park

With a bit of a foggy beginning Memorial Day has evolved into a three-day fun spree for most Americans. For me, as a child, it was our dad taking my brother and me to our mother's grave. We stood motionless in silence till dad turned for the car. Never a word was spoken.

We washed the cars while listening to the Indianapolis 500 on the radio. It was where our distant cousins, the Unsers, raced, often winning. Hot dogs and a few words about soldiers dying and that was the day.

As our country has been continuously at war for most all of my rather long life, Memorial Day seems just like another holiday.

The pain and human cost of the Civil War was the root of this day. Begun by General Logan in 1868, as Decoration Day to "strew flowers" at cemeteries to remember fallen comrades. The date was selected as no major battle occurred on May 30th.

By 1915, Moina Michael, the mother of the artificial red

poppies VFW's sold to aid orphans wrote: "We cherish too, the poppy red that grows on fields where valor led, it seems to signal to the skies that blood of heroes never dies."

Memorial Day was declared an official national holiday in 1971, and, unknown to most of us, a National Moment of Remembrance was added in 2000. At 3:00 p.m. the moment may be observed by listening to "Taps". This Memorial Day was different for me at the American Undersea Warfare Center on Pelican Island. Attending a moving ceremony, including the Tolling of the Bell and playing of "Taps" by USMC (Ret.) Art Vega standing on the bow of USS *Stewart*. Afterwards, I met the 1944 crew.

The captain of USS *Stewart*, ensign, chief petty officers, enlisted men, a WAVE, and Red Cross woman all spoke to me in person. "Captain" Bryan Fitch portrayed a lieutenant commander, a former reserve officer, in command of ninety-day wonders: new officers and former Coast Guard sailors. Destroyer escorts (DE) were built fast, in three months, and could be satisfactorily operated by rather inexperienced crews. That was the idea. DE's were needed to combat the German submarine wolf packs in the Atlantic during World War II.

Today people from all walks of life have brought the challenges and triumphs of these sailors to life in Seawolf Park. A fitting way to recreate and remember why there is a Memorial Day.

What's in A Name on the Wharf? The *General Rudder*

Always interested in who streets, buildings and ships are named after, the Texas A&M ship, *General Rudder*, moored at the far west end of the port, made me curious. The rudder causes a ship to maneuver—the larger the ship, the longer it takes to change direction. Maybe it is a term to help Texas A&M at Galveston Maritime Academy students remember the critical role a rudder plays?

A quick computer trip to Wikipedia provided the answer. General James E. Rudder, a Texan, lead American troops in a daring D-Day attack (as portrayed in *The Longest Day*) and later in the Battle of the Bulge. Beginning in 1959 until his death in 1970, he lead Texas A&M as president, guiding it from an agricultural school to a major university, admitting women and integrating the student body. President Rudder clearly fulfilled the definition of a ship's rudder, providing direction for troops and students.

After meeting some A&M students employed at the Texas Seaport Museum, I am interested in how the *General Rudder* connects to educating future ship mariners. Driving over the Pelican Island drawbridge, I saw the ship. Through the years various Texas clippers have tied up at A&M. (See Prof. Stephen Curley's books.)

Austin, a fitting name for an A&M student, met me right on time. He had set up this tour through Colonel Mallahan. Sharply dressed, Austin explains how he transferred from Clemson, where he majored in Chinese.

Heading up the gangplank, Austin described all of the activities. Maintenance is ongoing. Engineering students examine equipment, other students practice driving a forklift. On the bridge, another student summarizes his watch by writing in the logbook. Everyone paints.

Captain Joe Klenczar, A&M alumnus, greeted us in his boiler jumpsuit. Obviously, this is a hands-on captain. With patience, he walked this landlubber through the mission of the training ship. As a gifted instructor, combining theory with practice, he made me feel ready to go to sea. It was a shock to see that he passed away just after we met.

The captain clearly communicated educational philosophy and facts. About 50-60 students (about 10% women) per cruise, ranging from 15 to 80 days. Fifteen crew, including two cooks and four engineers. One day on a training ship equals one and half days towards a third mate's license. Students rotate every three days from actually running the ship to class- work.

Captain Klenczar told me the two biggest changes during his career are advances in technologies and increased safety. Students still need to learn to shoot the stars and operate the ship without computer assistance. While not a cruise ship, the quarters are nice with bunks and desks.

As interesting as the ship is, the students to me were the most impressive. These are not typical college students. Some are Navy ROTC. Some will become Merchant Mariners. All students follow a strenuous schedule and impressive curriculum necessary to safely operate large ships around the world. I think General Rudder would be proud.

Bow of General Rudder—notice the name was changed

Texas A&M at Galveston Cadets Sail the Seas

Like many wharf stories, this one began with a phone call from one of my new friends at the Port of Galveston. They asked, "Do you want to go aboard the Texas A&M at Galveston's *General Rudder*?" The next day I headed for Pier 21, where the *General Rudder* was tied alongside.

I paused at the bottom of the gangway. Two cadets were beginning to pull down some of the decorations.

"Are you all still giving tours?" I inquired.

"Yes, sir," Cadet Marwan Afify replied. "Come aboard, sir."

I must admit being called "sir" has a nice ring to it, even if undeserved.

Chief Mate Robert De Simone, second in command, kidded

with me. Every visit is always different as it's the people who bring the steel vessel to life. As the cadets proudly explained each aspect of the ship I gently asked questions. Becoming more comfortable, they abandon memorized words.

The Texas A&M at Galveston Maritime Academy flyer provided quotes from a diverse student body. Cassandra Sattler from Kansas said, "I was looking for an exciting career with world travel and great salaries." Corps Commander Rex Jones of Fredericksburg, home of Adm. Chester Nimitz, said, "Seeking an officer's commission in the U.S.Navy is opening the door to my future."Naval ROTC cadets may receive up to $8,000 per year and commit to serve after graduation. Who needs Annapolis?

Sara Ballard is a marine biology major from Fort Worth. Cameron Warden of Houston found A&M "a voyage of discovery."

"After two years in this program, I have crossed the Pacific Ocean four times," Ballard said.

My 22 days in the Caribbean on a cruise ship seems trivial.

Company Commander Ny' Eshia Murray of New Orleans is excited about entering a career in marine transportation. On the bridge Capt. Joe Klenczar, an A&M at Galveston graduate, explained they were getting underway the next morning. I joked, only slightly, that I was looking for a place to stow away.

He replied, "We are only off for a short cruise, down to Corpus."

My "Oh, that's fine with me," isn't met with an invitation. It is the season beginning for the *General Rudder* and 45 A&M at Galveston cadets.

Another 185 cadets gained experience on TS *Golden Bear,* including a transit through the Panama Canal where they viewed the new expansion. During construction,Ilya Espino de Marotta, an A&Malum, served as the highest-ranking woman in the Canal's 100-year history.

Tammy Lobaugh, the Maritime Academy's Executive Director for Operations, also made history as the first Aggie to serve as commandant of the TS *Golden Bear*. She sounded rightfully proud.

My educated guess is Texan General James E. Rudder, World War II and D-Day hero (see *The Longest Day*), today would be proudest of his time as president of Texas A&M. Under his leadership, women were admitted and the student body was integrated. Through these wonderful modern-day cadets, you see the results for our future.

Note: Capt. Joe Klenczar passed away a few months after this tour. A sad reminder to enjoy those who are with us while we can. He was a good man and mentor to many.

Even Palm Trees Volunteer at Seawolf Park

When there is something a little wrong with something does it always draw your eye? For me there is that blankety-blank volunteer palm tree growing out of the USS *Stewart's* hull amidships. It bothered me every time I drove up. Can you tell?

Today is the Big Event, a nationwide volunteer day for colleges. Texas A&M at Galveston Sea Aggies are going to help paint USS *Stewart* and other tasks. This included painting the shipping container where we store supplies.

The plan is to begin at 0900 hours—9 a.m. to me. As I arrived at the appointed time, I saw a swarm of NROTC Sea Aggies at work. They came early. Midshipman Asher Spalding opened up at 0600. I was in bed. Volunteers power the American Undersea Warfare Center at Seawolf Park. Unique partnerships provide a setting and experience only found here. The destroyer escort USS *Stewart*, and the submarine, USS *Cavalla*, sit next to each other. They shared an undersea war. Both were built during WWII, *Stewart* at the Brown Shipyard, just up the channel. *Cavalla* sank a Japanese aircraft carrier that had attacked Pearl Harbor, now 75 years ago.

A strong wind changes our painting plans. Not to mention large palm trees blocking our way growing out from under the shipping container.

With a crew of six, we planned and attacked. Not sure of my role, I began as a consultant, then background worker, cleaning away debris. Dewayne Davis, the AUWC Curator told me, "You don't have to do that kind of work." I replied, "I don't do idle well." I take a hacksaw to the palm fronds. They win a few rounds and soon I have bloody hands. Yes, I had gloves, but I loaned them out to one of the midshipmen.

Way before I thought we were ready, the consensus was to pull the palms out with a truck. After two trucks tried with no luck, the palms did not budge. Biting my tongue, there was no "I told you so." One young cadet kept calling "Austin." He bragged, "Austin can handle this." Who is Austin? The capitol? The founder of Texas?

Back to digging.

Soon a massive military six-ton truck arrived. A few minutes later, the palms were popped out and planted elsewhere in the park. Who was the legend behind the wheel?

Austin is from a long line of Maryland sailors. His grandfather was a Navy pilot. His dad is a Philly ship pilot, and Austin is studying to be a mariner at A&M. He bought the truck at Fort Riley in Kansas, put his car in the truck bed and drove down to Galveston. Austin's truck led the Veterans' half-marathon. He was in awe of their dedication. We were in awe of the truck.

Later, on a harbor tour, I saw the clean lines of USS *Stewart*, sans palm trees. Thank you, A&M cadets and the Big Event.

A Patriotic Untold Wharf Story

Everyone knows the story of Dunkirk. During the early days of World War II, the Nazi Blitz forced Allied armed forces in France to the edge of the sea. Over 350,000 British and French soldiers were trapped between overwhelming bombing and the English Channel. With a huge volunteer effort, they were rescued during nine long days by an "anything that could float" armada.

An even larger boatlift occurred in our recent lifetime, a story which has largely gone untold. Friends had emailed me a link claiming that over 500,000 people were rescued from wharves and most of us do not know about it.

Before opening the link, I thought of Asian ferries that have sunk with over 450 passengers on board. That's not it. What about the earthquake in Japan with the tsunami? No, the ocean was going the wrong direction to save people by sea. African refugees fleeing across the Mediterranean? Many, yet not the largest.

Finally, I'm thinking maybe this is a web hoax and my retired friends had been taken in? No, these are very sane friends.

Okay, time to open the link. We sort of knew this story, but other news over shadowed it. On 9/11 as the World Trade Towers fell, people fled to uptown New York, and 500,000 rushed a few blocks south to the tip of Manhattan, to the wharves. Trapped between a burning inferno and the water with nowhere to go, some jumped into the river, trying to swim. Panicked, others pushed toward the water as the towers crashed, shooting up giant clouds of smoke.

Instantaneously hundreds of tugs, ferries, fishing and pleasure boats raced toward the disaster. Boats driven by regular folks from all walks of life, all with one mission. Get half a million people off Manhattan. Rushing into the inferno, not knowing if another attack was coming, they returned over and over again. All bridges, tunnels and airports were closed. These boats were the only way off the island.

The Coast Guard asked all available boats to rendezvous on Governor's Island and let them know how many passengers they could carry. There were no regulations, rules or training that could have imagined this horror.

Everyone helped everyone. Boats from the *Amberjack* to the *Resolute* rushed back and forth. Morally, this was the right thing to do and Americans did it without regard to race, color, or sexual orientation.

As Romain Rolland said, "A hero is a man who does what he can." There were many heroes on 9/11. A half million dust-covered, zombie-looking New Yorkers were evacuated in only nine hours. Americans came together for the greater good. We know about that in Galveston. If only that feeling could have continued.

You can watch a powerful video about this on YouTube,

narrated by Tom Hanks: *BOATLIFT, An Untold Tale of 9/11 Resilience.*

Make History!

As we recognize 75 years since the bombing of Pearl Harbor, you can join the crew restoring USS *Stewart* and USS *Cavalla*. Both played critical roles during World War II. The submarine, USS *Cavalla*, sank one of the Japanese aircraft carriers that attacked Pearl Harbor. The *Cavalla* was present in Tokyo Bay at the war's end surrender ceremony. The destroyer escort USS *Stewart* was built and outfitted in Galveston Bay. She protected convoys bringing troops and critical war supplies to Europe and had just entered the Pacific at war's end.

We invite you to join a wonderful crew from all over the USA during Spring workweek at the American Undersea Warfare Center, Seawolf Park, on Pelican Island. Tasks include minor repairs, painting, working in the gift shop and everything in between.

Welcome aboard for a meaningful and historical experience. We have the best food in the fleet and you can sleep on board. Call 785-255-4368 with questions, or come by the Galveston Naval Museum, Galveston, Texas.

www.americanunderseawarfarecenter.com. Edsall Class Veterans Association Inc. A 501(C)3 Organization.

Chapter 10 – Seaports and Museums

Sailing Aboard the *Elissa*

Good morning, Jamie. Hi, Emma. Hey Wes, didn't know you were working today. Dee Dee, how are your boys? Do they know Mother's Day is coming up? Yes, they do and what to get. Mark, Morning, great day to sail.

Walking down the pier, a man reaches out to shake hands. "Hi, I'm John, great to meet you in person after all our emails."

My phone rings and I see my wife on the next wharf over. I begin walking that way toward the water when Richard, wearing a life vest, rushes over and says not to lean on the unlocked gate. Thanks, I don't need a swim before we sail.

Time to board the *Elissa*. Looking up from the gangway, the multicolored shirts are everywhere. The blue shirt crew is all up in the rigging. Three red shirted mast captains keep a close eye on every maneuver.

Rocky, a white-shirt officer, gives the safety lecture while we practice wearing wet life vests. First as a volunteer on the *Elissa*, now she is a professional sailor all over world including the South Pacific.

Captain Trost yells out nautical commands, a foreign language to me as the *Elissa* comes alive. Underway on the third oldest active sailing ship in the world, what a trip. The *Elissa* first visited Galveston in 1883 loaded with bananas, leaving with cotton.

Smoothly, we slide out into the Gulf of Mexico. Mitch, a middle-aged gentleman, climbs out on a wire over the bow to untie a sail. "Circus performers get paid for this," he volunteers.

LaDawn, a blue-shirt, completed 16 Saturdays of training. Beginning in complete confusion, eventually the 186 lines that allow the ship to move made sense.

Roy helped expert Jim Brink sew one quarter of an acre of canvas on the Ashton Villa ballroom floor, creating the 19 sails. Thirteen are set today, beautiful white clouds.

Staring up at the masts, with over two miles of tarred wire rigging and 4.5 miles of fiber rope, Jamie asks me what I think. Wow, it's like *Pirates of the Caribbean*.

Come to find out, he was the lead rigger on the last two *Pirates of the Caribbean* films and *The Bounty*, but this is real. His eyes light up even having sailed thousands of times as an officer on square-riggers before directing the Seaport Museum. This is better than a DVD—kids should love this!

After several hours, we come about and sail back towards Galveston, small on the horizon. Cookies are passed around and I allow myself a root beer. Everyone is involved in conversation. Kevin from Tyler does rust and oil changes. No strangers today. See Chris's video at www.galveston.com.

This 204-foot-long, 100-foot-tall steel-hulled machine, held together with rigging and decks of teak and Douglas fir, is far more than an 1877 iron barque, it is 30,000 of hours each year of fellowship. As amazing as the physical structure moving us over the sea, the *Elissa* is indeed a human experience. Stewardship of sails gone past makes for good friends, fair winds and a following sea.

Setting sail far above the deck

It's a Sailor's Life

Watching the bow wake foam quietly drifting by hypnotizes me as the officers ready the crew to return to Galveston. We have been transported to the 1800s aboard a tall ship. The *Elissa* is one of the rare barques still sailing. Erase the cell phone and folks wearing shoes and we are cruising a century ago.

Within the gunnels, the crew is busy coming about, turning the ship around. As lines are pulled across the deck a woman volunteer crewmember quickly curls the rope in a perfect circle. Try it sometime and you gain great admiration for this skill.

We sail into the Port of Galveston, heading for Pier 21, home of the Texas Seaport Museum, the *Seagull II* and the *Elissa*. In the 1800's docking a large sail ship in a rather narrow channel, current running about four miles per hour, was a challenge, even with dories (see the beautiful white one on the pier) pulling the ship alongside. Today a small engine aids the Captain and Mark, the bosun. They guide the crew in the rigging and the helmsman on the wheel aft. Standing close by, mesmerized by the interaction of the commands controlling the engineer and the wheelman, I soon hear a stern request from the Captain. He reminds me that as a guest, I belong starboard mid-ship, not in his line of sight in any direction. Oops! At least I was starboard.

The action is on the port (left) side as the ship's crew coordinates with the dockhands as the "python line"—huge woven ropes—are attached to the bow as we slowly drift by the pier. The python line stretches out slowing the ship to a stop. Quickly other lines secure us in just the right spot. Down goes the gangway.

The *Elissa* has completed another wonderful sailing season, yet it continues to educate and quicken the pulse of all who view her. Walking the dogs early one morning last weekend, I saw a number of cars parked inside the Seaport gate. I realized this must be a sleep-over for youth 9 - 14 years old who get to "bunk" before the mast for a day. Memories forever.

While the wind propels the *Elissa*, for free—nothing else about this cruise is. The volunteer crew supplies hundreds of hours of work each year, totaling over 28,000 hours. Even at rest, lines curving sculpted to the cleats wharf side, the *Elissa* emotionally moves us through the seas of history. With new educational ports to understanding waiting for us on every visit to the Texas Seaport Museum, who can resist?

Setting the Sail on *Elissa*

One of the first and most memorable wharf views is the *Elissa*, with three tall masts among the rigging. Waiting on Pier 21 for my Setting Sails workshop, I hear an approaching 7-year-old boy, "I want to be an entomologist, but I won't eat bugs." Where did that remark come from? We board with our instructor, Susan Vanderford (no relation to AC family). Susan begins with general facts about the ship. I look straight up to see men and women, working on the sails almost 100 feet above, balanced on a wire. Are they in the workshop, too? I promised I wouldn't put myself in danger, but it must be safe, so I mentally prepare to climb. This should make a good column, if I live.

Susan is explaining the triangle sail set on the deck in front of us. We will raise it by pulling on the rope, or line, in sailing terms, while standing on the deck. Relief, no climbing.

We queue up, line between us and the water for safety, and learn four naval terms required to raise the sail. After reading over forty books on sailing, "heave to" is the only one I really understand. After practice makes perfect, Susan cries out the commands and the sail begins to inch up the guideline. There are four of us: the 7-year-old, his mom and dad, and me in the rear. The couple are large and strong, and me large, but it still takes real effort to pull the line. This is like tug of war, and the ship is winning! With Mark, the bosun, and Richard's assistance the sail is set. If more than eight (out of a crew of 14) sailors were required, the capstan, a powerful winch, was used. Maybe three modern day adults should be the new standard.

Susan leads us before the mast (title of an 1835 good book by Dana) to the foc'sle bunkroom. Our young sailor asks about four-hour watches, port and starboard, and if there were bugs on the ship. "Yes," Susan answered, "but sailors did not have to eat them." Weevils came to mind, but I kept my mouth shut.

The workshop ends with a self-guided tour of the ship. Given some of my forehead DNA is already smashed on the hatches, I stay to visit with Susan about the experiential focus of the Texas Seaport Museum. Hired last month, she is designing and livening history along with STEM programs for schools and Sea Scouts. With an art history background and summers on her grandparent's 40-foot sloop, she is well qualified. Even exploring how to share the historic stench smell, something not on the website.

Returning to the deck, having experienced history, the young sailor excitedly tells Susan, "I thought this was going to be boring, but it is the best!" Yes, setting sail makes for a perfect afternoon—time for Starbucks.

A Library Day at Sea

Well, another mistake made in my life. For years, I taught the history of social welfare policy to hundreds of college students. The course included economics, employment, racism, family life, education, transportation and more. We had fun exploring social interactions from Babylon to Reagan. Don Perkins, a famous Dallas Cowboy role, played W.E. B. Du Bois in my class. The PBS American Experience films brought history to life along with some of my props. If only I had visited the fourth floor of the Rosenberg Library back then. Entering through the first-floor children's section is always fun. Then up the spiral staircase gazing at the sea mobile to the next floor to do research and buy a book or two.

With my wife's new knee, we had to take the elevator and by mistake ended up on the fourth floor. Here is the Galveston: Treasure Isle of the Gulf exhibit. Welcoming guests is a 12-foot-long model of SS (Steam Ship) *Indian,* which measured 482 feet, and sailed from 1900 to 1934. And that is only half the story, visit for the rest. Okay, the ship model is only a half, placed up against a mirror, making it appear as a full ship.

Down a few steps I am surrounded by displays tracing Galveston from the Karankawa, who I learn, used alligator oil for mosquito repellent—to the modern Port. Each case tells a story and presents artifacts donated by Galvestonians for over 100 years.

One display, "What's in a name?" tells how Bernardo de Galvez had San Luis Island renamed for him even though he never came near here. Jean Lafitte parked his pirates here until the U.S. Navy invited him to leave. Menard and Williams (no relation to my mother's side) settled the town, which grew to the Wall Street of the south before the 1900 storm.

The Texas Navies are on display along with the helm of the two USS Galveston ships, from 1905. Kids of all ages can spin the wheel while watching a large screen video tour of harbor sites.

A long list of Galveston firsts, include immigration with a Torah scroll and the first air conditioning in the USA placed in the Hollywood Dinner Club. Transportation across the causeway began in 1856, later allowing a one-hour train ride to Houston. Sigh.

Cotton was king and did Galveston ever profit from shipping it. Labor intensive, many African-Americans became experts in jamming bales into tight places and building a union.

This exhibit, donated by the Lykes family, provides more information and experiences per square foot than any library I have visited. And this is only one of four exhibits on this floor.

My notebook full, I begin to head up the few steps to leave. A retired couple standing at the top is debating whether to come down. "It is worth the steps and time," I suggest. Seeing them later they thank me, like excited school kids on a field trip.

Thank goodness for the wharves welcoming Henry Rosenberg, and for the library staff and the families for sharing our history. Riding the elevator to a new floor was a good mistake, even if a few years late.

Wharf History Exhibit Not to be Missed

"Boy! Don't you ever do that again." A white gas station man, dressed in all white, yelled at me as I emerged from a filthy Mississippi restroom. The year was 1964, not that long ago. The restrooms continued to be segregated, even after the Civil Rights Act was signed by LBJ. I had rushed into the "Colored" restroom. From New Mexico, I had no clue what he meant.

This memory came to mind while I viewed "Voices of the Past: An Exhibit Celebrating African-American History in Galveston" on the fourth floor of the Rosenberg Library. This emotional celebration of overcoming racism told by Galveston residents is available by phone: (409) 877-7899. Even my clam phone worked.

I was drawn to photo #17 of cotton jammers packing the hold of a sailboat. The voices of Ms. Fay Williams and Mr. Frederick Ferguson tell wonderful and shocking stories of the Galveston wharves. During Reconstruction, Jim Crow policies enforced segregation. From schools, bathrooms and beaches, to hospitals and drugstores, everything was separate and unequal through the 1960's.

Cotton Jammers Union Local 851, led by Ms. Williams' father, fought for equality, minimum wages and a 40-hour work week. Mr. Ferguson hauled 140-pound bundles, weighing the same as he did as a 16-year-old. Working 16 hours on Saturdays for time-and-a-half, he was able to finance part of his college education.

African-American wharf workers began the Cotton Jammers Union after they were recruited to break a white union strike. According to 91-year-old Mr. D. J. Crainer, they were refused membership in the Screwmen's Benevolent Association until a court settlement in 1983.

The Hispanic union, working mainly produce shipments, also was included in the settlement. Black union workers lost seniority in the merger, taking many years to gain equality. Now, 150 years after the Civil War, at last, union officers are from all cultures and all friends. Mr. Reggie Clark followed his father as a Longshoreman. When there were two unions, white and black, they took turns; front three ship holds one time and then the back two. Both he and Ted O'Rourke credit unions for creating the middle class in Galveston. Most Black churches were built with Longshoremen's money, Mr. Clark surmises.

The exhibit will be available online and as a traveling exhibit, serving as a powerful reminder of the racism used to build our city. An important reminder for today's world.

Nautilus and Texas Frontier in Ocean Exploration

Receiving a cryptic tip that the *Nautilus* is at the Port, thoughts race through my mind. How did a 1955 nuclear submarine slip past the City Council? Submerged? No, the channel is too shallow.

Wait, *Nautilus* (from Jules Verne) is now the name of Dr. Bob Ballard's (discovered the *Titanic*) research vessel. Wikipedia confirms I'm correct, and *Nautilus* is in Turkey? No, I just saw it at Pier 26 this morning and on the front page of the paper.

Checking their superb website (nautiluslive.org), I see that the Malin Yard, where the *Sturgis* is docked, repaired the critical aft wench which allows the ship to launch its four ROV's (robot subs). Traveling to the Gulf to "cure" the new cable, stretching it out 4,000 meters, they returned to Galveston to entertain STEM students. The live video feed provides real-time 'round-the-clock action—crystal clear pictures from thousands of feet below the sea, from U-boat shipwrecks to crustaceans.

I wish I could visit these dynamic folks and, poof, the Port quickly arranges a visit. Arriving, I look up and see a nice young "sailor" on the rail of the *Nautilus.* I inquire where check-in is, and he responds, "Whom are you seeing?"

"Dr. Dwight Colman."

He breaks into a big smile. "Welcome aboard, that is I."

First, I get a full tour, including examining the ROVs, *Argus,* and the two-ton *Hercules* and standing in the control van where the ROV's are operated, to video and collect samples guided by scientists watching TVscreens. Passing the gym, hot tub and multinational crew's quarters, I realize this small ship is an exceedingly complex operation. Technology is everywhere: computer rooms, labs, ROV hangars, workshops, production studio.

Settling down in the exquisite wood-trimmed lounge (completed in Turkey), Dr. Coleman explains the mission of the expedition with a slight New England accent. Studies on volcanoes, rocks, and bacteria eating away shipwrecks, to salinity and how Texas A&M-Galveston, Texas State University, and NOVA work with the University of Rhode Island and Harvard. And he tells me the sub, *Alvin,* is named for Allyn Vine, not me. Shucks!

Dr. Coleman became an oceanographer through encouragement from his grandmother, together with an interest in the sea, maps, and National Geographic magazines. Joining Dr. Ballard in 1999, he now is an expedition leader, overseeing teacher ambassadors, interns and a crew of scientists and technicians on the *Nautilus* six months and completing reports and grant proposals the rest of the year. Oh, and he directs the Inner Space Center at URI, too.

The ship leaves for the Panama Canal and the Pacific without Dr. Coleman aboard. His son is graduating from high school. As exciting as the trips are, family comes first.

Walking off the beautiful wood gangway, I leave as many visitors do, engaged, better educated, eager to collaborate and certainly inspired—I think Dr. Ballard and the Ocean Exploration Trust should be pleased.

Orphans, Wharves and Tom Lea

My favorite (made me look good) football receiver, John, grew up in an orphanage. His mother died and his father, in the Merchant Marines, was gone for months at a time.

Galveston had a similar orphanage, designed by Albert Muller and funded by Henry Rosenberg in 1895. Damaged in the 1900 storm, all children survived. Following repairs, it was home for hundreds of children who lost mothers or fathers, often to the sea, until 1984. After sitting empty, the home transitioned to the Bryan Museum, located at 1315 21st Street, just down from the Galvez Hotel. As a former social work professor, my interest in and research of the children and building is years long.

Hearing great things about the collection and remodeling from my friends "Margaret" Lynette and John Moore, nothing prepared me for the architecture, artwork or presentation. Walking in a light rain through the garden, up the grand stairway I am greeted by a volunteer, "Are you here for the tour?" Smiling broadly in my blue striped seersucker suit with green bowtie and black boots, I think, "You don't know how ready."

The noble front door swings open and our first docent, Barbara, a past colleague at University of Houston-Downtown, welcomes us. A side door opens to a view out of a Disneyland ride, except this is all real. We see a large Spanish Galleon model and Bernado de Galvez himself.

Docent Don points out a stone bowl 9,000 years old amid several Native American items tracing the history of Galveston. Other interesting stories include my supposed relative, La Salle (possible distant relative?), who made "dubious" attempts to settle Texas before the Spanish.

The next docent, a former 12-year-old cowboy, provides details of the 1800's era saddles, spurs, famous guns and an assassination fiddle. This large room is full of historical firearms.

Down the wide hall, formerly the second-floor boy's dorm, is now the library. Standing beside a Texas size table, Shelby explains the documents available. What a nice reading room for column writing research.

In the art gallery, Tom Lea III appears, smiling down on us. Among several Lea drawings is the Sam Houston painting with a long rifle. Set to be issued November 22, 1963, as a stamp, it was delayed.

Other Texas artists' works are here, too. The 1885, "Above the Falls of the Pedernales" by Lungkwitz, breathes coolness.

Taking the orphan children's worn wood back steps to the basement I am eager to see the kid's area. Entering, the 5'10" Ashley suggests that at 6'3", I duck. The ceiling is lower here in the children's domain. Under the stairs is a kid's secret old hangout with toys and games—adults don't fit. A display case holds caseworkers notes from 1927 with guidelines for abusive or poor parents.

Bending under a giant octopus into a wharf-themed theater, I hear Jan describe how school groups will watch a Galveston movie, then move to the pirate ship for review. Correct answers receive smoke rings blasted from the cannon.

The Bryan blends the past to future lessons though the world's largest collection of Southwestern art, artifacts and scholarship, all in a wonderful warm space. Mrs. and Mr. Moses Austin would be proud of their Bryan descendant's exhibition in Galveston.

An Old Box of Ship Medicines is History Today

Standing in a large conference room with wood paneled cases the temperature is 68, and humidity 45 percent on a hot late spring day. It doesn't look like a hurricane-proof vault, yet it is.

Across the room, I spy a wooden box. About two feet square, it is clearly old and well built. I see neat hand-cut dovetail joints. Tenons fit tightly in the corner notches—mortises. Perfect and precise making them valuable.

Robert Marlin swings the front doors of the cabinet open revealing bottles, snug in boxes built into the doors and main section. Hand-blown glass decanters from the 1800's contain pharmaceuticals.

"Everything a ship's pharmacy mate would need over the course of a long cruise is contained in this box," Marlin explains. While there were steam-powered ships during this time, they still were tossed about in rough seas, thus the tightly packed delicate medical cargo.

Mr. Marlin, a certified archivist, knows what he is talking about. As the archivist for the University of Texas Medical Branch (UTMB), he oversees the collection of over 20,000 rare books and artifacts related to medicine. From B.C. to 16th-century ivory dolls, which come apart to reveal organs, to million-dollar books and the best collection of NASA health-related papers, they are all here.

Without the Galveston wharf's commerce, the Texas policy-makers would not have pursued a world-class university in 1839. It took a while, but in 1891 "Old Red" was built and University of Texas Medical Branch opened.

A hospital across the street had just been constructed straight from the drawing on the desk of Nicholas Clayton. I know because Mr. Marlin showed me the actual plans. It is a beautiful painting, with blue watercolor windowpanes. A photo would not do it justice. Like masterpieces, you need to see in person.

In Dr. Boor's book *The Ice Merchant*, cadavers, which students used to learn medical practice, were allegedly brought to the new college in the 1890's from New England.

The labs held yellow fever samples, just as today. Another building, we are not allowed to visit, with good reason, contains Zika and Ebola. UTMB is still leading in healthcare.

UTMB values the past, not just for historical reasons, but also to continue to discover cures and best practices. "In 200 years, medical students will be studying what UTMB is doing in computer assisted surgery right now," Marlin said.

UTMB's History of Space Medicine collection is the gold standard for space health issues. It's often accessed to answer questions, such as why NASA Astronaut Scott Kelly grew two inches in space over his year-long stay. My guess of Pilates is incorrect.

Kevin Haslam, who is Senior Director and Assistant Vice President of Development, keeps his eyes open for additions to the collection, as he meets with alums and friends of UTMB. One alum contributed a complete set of syllabi and notes from his 1950's medical education at UTMB. He even had them bound. A snapshot of medical knowledge development is held in those dozen large volumes.

As a former Prof. I say, "Wow!"

An Utterly Wonderful Afternoon Cruise

A three-hour Saturday afternoon cruise for a few bucks sounds good to me. A phone call to (409)572-2561, and the woman quickly books the trip. "Be at Sea Star Base Galveston (SSBG) at 12:30 p.m.," she says.

"No problem," I reply. "See you then."

Saturday morning I'm off to Seawolf Park for a simple repair job on USS *Stewart* with Mike Vigneault. Several hours later the ship reminds us there are no easy fixes on a 73-year-old ship.

Home at noon, I relax. Was there something else to do today? Oh! The cruise. It's 12:30 already. I head straight to the boat. It is 12:40 p.m.

Standing on the gangway is a smiling fit gentleman dressed like a "Below the Decks" captain on a luxury yacht: pressed shorts, white shirt with stripes. "Hi, I'm Capt. Keith," he says.

"I'm late." I reply.

"No problem. Island time."

After a briefing, we cast off, motoring down the Bayou behind Moody Gardens, and heading for the Intracoastal Waterway. Capt. Cassidy Brown answers our questions. She has spent two years gaining experience here, the epitome of SSBG.

The capacity of the *BaySmart Express* is one hundred guests. This "pre-summer shakedown" trip will advertise the tour with banners on each side.

The boat is really nice. There are comfortable seats in a lecture room-type configuration with large screen TV for instruction. The AIS is on. It tracks every commercial boat in the area. The water is packed full of boats.

At 111-feet long, with a beam of twenty feet, *BaySmart* is roomy—three decks including a berthing area for eighteen. Except for the engine room, the boat is open to explore. Of course, I dash to the bridge to see all the action. It is an air-conditioned, leather-seated, high-tech center with a real wheel.

His head on a swivel, Capt. Keith Roberts is at the helm. As we enter the channel, he explains the complexity of the scene, motorboats racing past, teenagers at the controls, and barges that can't maneuver.

Capt. Keith is an able retired nuclear submariner and Coast Guard navigator. Besides driving an icebreaker, he once set a course from Hawaii to Alaska using only the stars.

Carol, his wife, is along for the ride. She heads communications at American National Insurance, which is in the tallest building in Galveston. Surprisingly, both are from New York, and yet they met in a Belfast pub. It's a small world after all. They moved to Bayou Vista to be near the water. Actually. The head of their bed is only 20 feet from the Bayou, I am told.

Senior Captain Margaret Candler enters the bridge, sharing the mission and history. "An exciting voyage of marine discovery," awaits kids and adults alike through educational programs from sailing to STEM.

Leaving *BaySmart* at the wharf, I visit for a while with a retired College Dean from Dallas. "Write that it was an utterly wonderful afternoon," he said. Yes, indeed it was, and hopefully there will be many more. For more information visit: www.SSBGalveston.org.

Chapter 11 - Other Wharves

A View from the Dock in Istanbul

The 15 July Martyrs Bridge over the Bosporus Strait in Istanbul, Turkey, has been on TV this past week. Connecting Europe with Asia, this strait is a fitting symbol of Turkey, attempting to link the Middle East with the West, the past with the future and democracy with security.

Just three years ago, I stood on the ferry dock eager to view this modern city of 18 million people from the water. What a voyage. For ten very full days we met with educators, business and healthcare leaders, families and the media. With 8,000 years of history and the birthplace to almost all western civilizations, the story of Turkey is as complex as the restored ancient cities and wonders we visited.

Change here is constant, so any snapshot assessment will be blurred. Turkey's picture today is again unclear.

During our visit, we met reporters from the country's "*NY Times*" and "*NBC*" television network. One bright, determined young woman reporter with a scarf over her head, as a symbol of independence, spoke of the challenges covering the government. A TV anchor person in a studio faultlessly reading the teleprompter in Turkish, paused during a commercial break to tell us about Texas, in perfect English. Both said, "We love the USA."

Now President Erdogan has shut down media outlets. Under the guise of threats of terrorism, Erdogan appears to be moving to centralize more power, crushing freedoms and dissents.

Erdogan is trying to entangle the U.S. in his political spider's web, threatening that if the US doesn't hand over his main opponent, Fethullah Gulen, living in exile in the US, our strategic agreements will be ended.

This after President Obama (he knew) backed Erdogan during the coup attempt. Erdogan is now blaming the U.S. for the coup? How reckless.

Gulen, who advocates peace similar to Gandhi, condemned the coup immediately and denied any involvement. His institute, a non-profit research organization, is dedicated to promoting of peace and democracy.

The Gulen Institute (www. guleninstitute.org) is housed at the University of Houston. Its mission is strongly counter to a violent coup or the dismantling of a democratic country.

At the conclusion of our visit in Turkey, our host, a proud retired autoworker, quietly spoke to us. He thanked us for visiting his country and assured us he and his family wished the USA the very best as the world leader.

He wanted nothing from us but understanding and friendship. His fivegrown children are all university graduates, fluent in English and one is a U.S. citizen. The father's only request was that we not give in to our fears and prejudices. He asked that we not deny his family visits and work in the U.S.

Trump was not on the horizon three years ago, but the father already felt the unfair message against all Muslims. We cannot afford to lose Turkey as an ally, and Turkey cannot afford to lose freedoms by becoming a dictatorship under the veil of security.

Bosporus Strait in Istanbul

The Last Ship Out of Cherburg

"We were on the last ship out of Cherburg 1939." A cold chill went up my spine. "Let me show you." Our close friend of ten years, Marilyn, leafed through a large old photo album. "Here is the last photo taken of my family. It was Passover 1939." A large, handsome extended family, from 3-year-old Marilyn to grandfathers.

At my request, she began the story. Her grandfather had moved to Pandelys, Lithuania, a town of five hundred in the region between Germany and Russia.

Marilyn's father, Velvul, later known as William, was drafted into the Russia Army at the outbreak of World War I. Contracting malaria while posted in the Caucasus Mountains, he missed the bitter fighting. He learned, while recuperating in the hospital, that his hometown had been captured by Germans. His reaction was that life would be better under the Germans than the Russians, a tough choice to me.

Having returned to his home, he was out in his garden one day when a German officer rode by on his horse. William looked up and said hello in German. The officer was surprised to hear a

Lithuanian villager speak German, not to mention six other languages. Long story short, the general selected William to be the mayor, the bergermeister for the village.

One day, the general asked William to help find a pair of white horses to buy for his wife. William did.

A poor farmer had his all his stock taken by the German soldiers. William intervened on his behalf, and the general had the stock returned unharmed. Overjoyed, the farmer sent William fresh dairy products each week for free. Over the years, the farmer became wealthy, sending all his children to college.

The Germans left at the end of the war in 1918, but William's legacy offairness remained. By 1939, the winds of war were blowing again. The former general contacted William and said, "It is not a good time for your people. You need to leave the country now."

The family applied for immediate U.S. immigration, which was given in 1946. With assistance from the poor farmer's son, now a government minister, documents were obtained and friends in the U.S. got the date moved up to 1939. After a harrowing trip through Germany and France, six members of the family boarded the last ship to make it out before Germany attacked.

I looked at the photo—there must have been twenty people staring at me.

"We don't know what happened to the rest of the family," Marilyn said. "We know others in the village pointed out the Jews when the Nazis invaded. In this town of five hundred friends, the Jews were rounded up, placed in the square, doused with gasoline and set afire, while their neighbors jeered."

As she finished, exhausted, I whispered, "People need to know this story."

"Why?" she asked.

Two weeks later the President of the United States said there were fine people on both sides in Charlottesville.

A True Immigration Story

The early sunlight streaked across the wide sandy beach, used boats being readied. Eight-year-old Matthew headed off to school as his parents prepared to go fishing. It looked and sounded like another great day on the Gulf Coast. Yet, within a year, this boy became the perfect weapon in the meanest wars in the world—a child soldier in Africa.

His mother died, and his father could not afford to pay for his school. He began to fish with his dad. Seven months later, his father passed away.

Forced to live on the streets, Matthew struggled to barely survive. Then, with some of his friends, he was attacked and taken by a gang. He was forced to join a rebel rag tag army in a neighboring country. One of his friends refused to fight, and the other boys were forced to kill him or be killed.

Over 300,000 children in African conflicts were used as weapons. Children are easily manipulated, intensely loyal, fearless and in endless supply. As a strong young 10-year-old, Matthew was perfect for the rebels' purposes. He was fed. He was trained, threatened and forced into combat with a light automatic rifle.

After several years of this hell, Matthew and two friends made a run for it. As he ran as fast as he could, shots rang out. One of his friends was hit. Matthew ran even faster.

Making his way back to his country, he worked the streets to raise enough money to be smuggled on a ship as a stowaway. After paying a large sum to a "friend" he was led forward and lowered into the anchor chain locker on a large cargo ship. As the chain was raised and washed off it was dropped into a deep dark steel container. Matthew curled up on the cold steel. He could hear another boy weeping in the other locker.

Two days out at sea he was found and taken to the captain. Afraid he would be thrown overboard, as he had heard other kids were, he was relieved to simply be locked in a cabin. The captain's wife was aboard for the trip. She visited Mathew and partly understood his story. When they reached Miami, she helped deal with immigration.

Locked up again, in the next few years, he was transferred to

Chicago to Houston to Conroe and to Galveston. Each time in this complex bureaucratic maze, he feared he was going to be sent back to Africa. And he cried, a strong young man, who had seen the worst in humankind, sobbed in fear of what the U.S. government might do to him.

Through the efforts of several lawyers, working for free, he came to the Children's Center in Galveston.

Visiting with Matthew several times, I found him a thoughtful, open young man with dreams of teaching math. After years in U.S. facilities, watching hours and hours of television, he speaks almost perfect English, not his native tongue.

Just last week, he learned he has been awarded his U.S. residency status. If ever a young man met the requirements for asylum, it is Matthew.

His long journey is surely not over—he will have flashbacks and more challenges to overcome. Yet, he is happy that at age 17 he is able to have the resources of the Children's Center in Galveston, including the immigration expertise of President Terry Keel. Very few of the other 300,00 child soldiers are so blessed.

Today children are routinely torn from their parents' arms and put behind fences, some lost in the system—not in Africa, but here in Texas. All by politicians who support family first.

It Could Have Been Galveston

"You know Mr. Martinez almost began his business in Galveston." A young man with a Panama hat smiled at me when I looked up from reading a poster. We were in a nice small museum in downtown Ybor City, a section of Tampa. "Hi, I am Max Herman of Ybor City Historic Walking Tours. Yes, his whole cigar making factory would have been wiped out in 1900 if he had located in Galveston." he added. Thus began an interesting and totally unexpected conversation.

I was in Ybor City spending a few minutes before departing on an airplane, which should have been a ship, sailing to Key West and Havana. Out in the Atlantic a Cat 5 hurricane was brewing yet no threat to me. No, it was a phone call. "Mother fell again. You'd better come fast," my brother said.

A call to Southwest on this Labor Day afternoon, a brief explanation, a long hold and then, "We have you booked on the next flight to Albuquerque. It leaves in four hours," the woman said.

So I walked the few sort of familiar streets of Ybor City—7th Street, to be exact. I had been here briefly many years ago, just a drive-by sight on the way from a meeting downtown.

The street has the similarity of the Strand of a few years ago, before the Mitchell magic touch. Restaurants here and there, a t-shirt shop, old-time drug store and vacant buildings waiting for the prince. A busy street, the beat of Cuban music from car trunks bounced off the walls and shimmied down your spine. A few streets over was a block-long tall red brick 1900's-era building. A non-sequitur sign read, "Church of Scientology". Must be a story here and there was.

Mr. Vicente Martinez-Ybor, born in Spain, moved to Cuba to avoid the draft in the 1830's. By the late 1850's he had his own cigar brand, famous even today to any college kid of the 1960's: Prince of Wales.

Ten years later, the revolution forced Martinez-Ybor to Key West. Key West served as a pause for his factory. Labor unrest and transportation problems forced him to look elsewhere. The elsewhere was Galveston, a booming city entering the 1880's.

Yet a sleepy little Florida village named Tampa, which was served by a rail line and a new port, all in a very humid environment (necessary for cigar-making) plus a $5,000 subsidy, won out. Galveston lost.

Martinez-Ybor encouraged his competition to join him there, creating a large Cuban labor pool. The industry provided fair wages, at-cost homes, healthcare and social services. Soon the city grew, as did production—millions of cigars by the 1920's.

What a pleasant few hours' distraction. Later that week sitting next to Mother in hospice care, I saw the streets Ybor City awash on television. I wonder, how is my new friend Max? (www.yborwalkingtours.com)

Port of Call Checklist

Always enjoying research, my recent cruise to Key West, a four-by-six-mile island, provides a perfect opportunity to study a Port of Call. Having lived in Key West when I was a few months old, while Dad was on active duty in the Navy, and visiting a few times since, I looked forward to a Mallory Square sunset, the Truman White House and other sites.

Now thanks to Bill Love and Mike Mierzwa's columns on Galveston as a Port of Call I employed a new perspective. I asked everyone I met in Key West what they thought about being a Port of Call.

The ship arrived at 10 a.m. After waiting about twenty-five minutes in the stairwell we walked out on the dock. With two thousand confused shipmates we are seeking the correct tour paddle held over guide's heads. Locating our ship's excursion salesperson, I asked where we needed to be. He directed us to a soon-to-be gathering spot for the six-mile bike tour. In another fifteen minutes or so, Denison appeared with the magic paddle.

Now the most important question: where are the restrooms? There is one about a block away, with one stall. More waiting. First impression? Not good.

Time to head out. Even at 6'3", I strained to keep the weaving paddle in view during the two-block walk through morning traffic and crowded sidewalks. We stumble along with no idea where we are going.

Poof. Old school bikes appeared. The bikes, with back pedal brakes, confuse the folks under thirty. They had no clue how to stop.

It was great gliding by the old Navy yard, where I lived 65 years ago, over to Hemingway's home, through interesting neighborhoods and to the southern-most home in the U.S.A. Back at the shop, our guide pointed the direction of other points of interest and needs, such as the drug store and where to eat local.

Based on my experience, critical factors for a Port of Call in Galveston are: calm, friendly local folks who listen and want visitors to have a wonderful experience in their town. A smooth flow of passengers go wherever they want to go, including great local and fast food service. Disneyland has this down cold—maybe more research is required?

And a full range of activities, from history to thrills for all abilities. In Galveston, we have fishing, duck boat, harbor and twister boat rides, and walking, electric cart, and bus tours to art galleries, homes, aquariums, swim-up hotel bars and the Pleasure Pier. We need enough clean restrooms, though. One small trailer won't cut it.

On a legal note from a non-attorney: I was told the U.S. Jones Act appears to prohibit ships registered in foreign countries from sailing from one U.S. port directly to another U.S. port. The cruise lines get around this in Key West by not "disembarking" any passengers. New Orleans, Bahamas, Galveston? Otherwise: check, check, check. Galveston would be a great Port of Call.

California Wharves

Boarding the train in Albuquerque at 5:25 p.m. we are just in time for the first dinner sitting. After dinner, a visit to the scenic car for the sunset over the red cliffs of Gallup, New Mexico.

We return to our cabins to find the beds turned down. Up at 5:25a.m, for the first and only breakfast sitting. The sun wakes up over the edge of Cajon Canyon, as we slowly snake our way down to sea level. Later we learn a forest fire caught a number of autos on fire in the canyon. Disembarking in LA's beautifully restored Union Station, we set off to find the rental car. This is a relative vacation, as Nicole, our granddaughter, states. That is, to see relatives, not theme parks.

Cruising down I-5, with 14 lanes of concrete, no orange barrels in sight and the HOV lane entrance is right here, not off in some neighborhood. Smooth. Flowers and trees line the freeway all the way to San Clemente, our first wharf. Well, actually a pier.

"It never rains in Southern California but girl, don't they warn ya, it pours, man, it pours (Albert Hammond)," dances in my head as I strain to see out the windshield. We find an "indoor" (separate buildings) Ocean Institute in Dana Point with lots of hands on experiences for the girls and benches on which to visit with our relatives. That night for the first time in years the Angels baseball game is rained out.

When the rain stops, we walk the long wooden planked pier, watching large waves and wetsuited surfers below. A gorgeous 1947 Ford Woody piques my interest and surfer tunes enter my ears. Later the girls venture to the edge of the cold, rocky beach waves. No gentle slope here, just a drop off into a rip tide. With cousin's buckets the girls make great sand castles. There is a lifeguard stand, but no guard. They need a Captain Davis.

Next day we head down the I-5 to San Diego to the aircraft carrier, USS Midway. Across the bay on Coronado Island, we see two modern carriers.

The Midway is a state of the art display, with hologram men from WWII describing the six minutes that won the war in the Pacific at Midway, to exquisitely restored cabins and a great café on the fantail. The four-acre flight deck holds a dozen planes and displays with retired seamen explaining tail hooks to catapults.

With over 700 volunteers, a retired admiral as the CEO, and support from several corporations, this huge ship shines. With CPO Mac's eyes, however, I spot some rust where tourists don't normally look. Rust doesn't sleep even aboard this striking ship.

What a wonderful few days in SoCal. On the way to the airport, I ask Nicole, should Grandpa move to San Diego? No, she quickly answers, stay in Galveston. Well, gas is not $4.25 and parking at the Galveston Wharf doesn't cost $16, no rainouts at Astros games and the waves are warm. This eight-year-old makes sense.

Source of Dana Point, California, Wharves Found

Staring out at the delightful Dana Point Harbor, paddle-boarders gliding over the smooth water, I am distracted by a group of kids in blue Ocean Institute shirts. Nicole and I came for the Institute's tour. The tour was truncated to accommodate the last summer camp session. The Ocean Institute is a nationally known marine science and history educational center for thousands of students and teachers.

My attention returned to our guide, Laura, as she pointed out the *Pilgrim*, an 86-foot-long, 1835 three-masted sailboat, tied to the wharf. The name and date rang a bell somewhere in the depths of my memory.

Right, Richard Henry Dana's boat. The author of *Two Years Before the Mast*, Dana visited this very point on his voyage from Boston around Cape Horn up the Californian coast and back in 1835.

Laura asked if any of us knew his story. I explained, at her request, some history of this unusual, largely unknown gentleman.

As a Harvard student, he was stricken by measles his junior year. It affected his eyesight. He took to the sea as a cure. A courageous young man, he chose the role of a common sailor, housed before the mast, the worst part of the ship.

His journal of the trip reads like poetry. In fact, Herman Melville wrote that Dana's description of rounding the Horn could have been written with an icicle. Brrr.

In chapter two Dana wrote: "The wind was whistling through the rigging, loose ropes flying about; loud and, to me, unintelligible orders constantly given and rapidly executed, and the sailors 'singing out' at the ropes in their hoarse and peculiar strains. In addition to all this, I had not got my 'sea legs on,' was dreadfully sick, with hardly strength enough to hold on to anything, and it was 'pitch dark.' This was my state when I was ordered aloft, for the first time, to reef topsails."

The purpose of the voyage was to obtain cowhides from this section of what was then Mexico. Speaking Spanish, Dana headed the buying and transporting of the hides to the vessel.

After purchasing the hides for one dollar a piece (thus the term "buck") at the Mission San Juan Capistrano, the challenge was how to get them to the beach. Most of coastline here has high cliffs—headlands. Very steep, as we found hiking up from

Strand Beach below the Ritz Carlton Hotel.

Dana's solution was to spin the hides off the bluff like a Frisbee. Today the hide "drogher" (porter) statue depicting Dana's tosses rests at the base of Violet Lantern Lane above the harbor.

The Mission, just over the hill from my cousin's modern home, still remains home to the swallows. A quiet, small village, frozen in the 1700's, complete with a petting zoo, visited by the 21st-century iron horse several times a day.

How would Dana describe his namesake today? Wow, what a difference a couple of hundred years makes. It is as though the greater metropolitan area has been gently laid over California's history.

Van, Bus, Planes, Bikes & Trains to California Coast

Turning to my good friend Bill Flores, I said, "Can't believe we are driving through Los Angeles at seventy miles an hour." Of course it was 12:30 a.m. on the 210 to the 101.

Keeping freeway numbers straight is harder than trying to remember passwords. Around SoCal, it's "take the 5 to the 57, off on the 91 and you're there." At least there is a plethora of road signs.

Months ago, I'd offered to drive the rental van for Bill from Houston to California. I ended up in Albuquerque on the day he left H-town, so we met in the Duke City.

The plan was to drive to Flagstaff for the night and then go into Santa Barbara the next day. As the conversation energized us, we sailed over the mountains of Arizona and downhill so easy we couldn't bear tostop.

A 14-hour visit with a long-time friend beginning a new job as president of a university in his home state provided enough material to discuss later into the night. Pulling up in front of Bill's new home, we inhaled the fresh sea fragrance of the Pacific fog. Nothing like it. The next morning, we unloaded clothes at his home, and books and paintings at his new office in downtown Santa Barbara. We were in walking distance to anything you would need. We needed lunch and massages.

Lunch was under an umbrella on the sidewalk and massage next door. All in the cool 82 degrees and 30 percent humidity in the coastal breeze. Locals decried the heat wave. Really?

That afternoon with his wife, Noel, and her mother and their kids, we explored the picturesque Mission, large pier, museums and private beach. Each Disneyland perfect.

Bill picked-up the tab for everything. Occasionally I saw the price—this place isn't cheap. Many homes are bought as interest only, almost like renting. Salaries are not high enough for million-dollar tract homes.

Given that we had arrived in California early, I looked for a train or plane to leave sooner. No luck, Amtrak required double the early-bird price, so the train left with empty cabins.

Bill wanted to drive me the 90 miles to LAX, but I knew that could be a six-hour roundtrip, so I gave him a firm no and booked the bus then the plane.

The next week our son Charles and granddaughter Nicole and I headed back to SoCal on the train. Charles did a triathlon with my cousin Mike at Camp Pendleton, swimming in the cold tossing ocean. The only boat we got on was a huge Navy hovercraft, which served as the finish line.

Charles had to fly to Chicago for a meeting, leaving me to bring Nicole and his bicycle back on the train. Commuter trains seem to run on time and made connections easy.

Then a flight back to Galveston and home. This is retirement? I am beat. Maybe I need a new approach. A cruise maybe?

Looking for A Wharf in Santa Fe, New Mexico

Crystal clear mountain air with a hint of fall softly flowed through the car window. Meandering through narrow pinon-covered hilly roads, I watched for home number eight on the Hacienda Parade. The Parade of Homes in Santa Fe. Understand, there is no straight street in Santa Fe, the "City Different." No rectangular Galveston city blocks with numbers orletters.

Spotting a small sandwich board sign I turned up a winding

trail to a dead-end. Tucked into the hillside, home number five. Oh well, it looked nice, so tour time.

Through the eight-foot carved wooden door was an exposed adobe wall on the left. The concrete floors were so cool, almost cold under my bare feet. Sight was drawn to the classic Taos school-style paintings which coursed up the 12-foot-high walls. Vigas—logs spaced three-feet-apart held up the ceiling. Pueblo style all the way. The space calmed one, similar to driving across the causeway.

An involuntary "ah," a physical and psychological relaxation.

Every portal offered an ever-changing landscape portrait. Georgia O'Keeffe puffy white clouds in turquoise skies floated over mountains in every direction. Opened windows with the 68-degree morning August breeze whispering through.

Wandering into the large open kitchen, eyes focused out the double window over the sink, in my peripheral vision I saw an attractive woman with silver short sculptured hair wiping the counter. She smiled with a hint of recognition.

"I'm Alvin," I said, then it clicked. "Carmen?" I inquired. "Alvin," she exclaimed. Turned out this was Carmen and Rick's new home. We worked together at New Mexico State University 10 years ago.

Last month on my drive to California with our mutual friend and former boss Dr. Bill Flores told me about Carmen Gonzales' home in detail. A LEED Platinum home, the first such in Santa Fe. Beautiful and efficient.

Carmen caught me up on life, friends and retirement—we both tried it the first time for only a few days. A personal tour of the home revealed details. The huge garage had to be detached to achieve LEED rating due to the risk of carbon monoxide leak. Important detail.

We headed out as the home filled up with folks, their jaws dropping at each vista. From Bill's description, I had thought the home was further north in another neighborhood. Home number eight was north in an old school converted to condos, two classrooms-size each. Talk about a huge bedroom.

Just down the road I heard the gurgle of water. Looking over a rusted railing (yes, rust even in the high desert) I saw a dense grove of small trees. A petite sign read, "Santa Fe River".

The river's width here was about five feet. Hey, all of us began small. It runs off the 7,000-foot mesa into the Big River, known as the Rio Grande, through Cochiti Lake, then all the way to Gulf of Mexico and the wharves of Galveston. We live in a connected world for sure.

A Port in the Desert?

In a comfortable air-conditioned Community College auditorium, a group of group of mostly men are sitting on the stage around tables. Name placards identify each as a state senator or representative. At a facing table, the New Mexico State Police Chief is testifying.

The chief mentions how security has been increased at the ports. I look up from the manuscript I'm editing. Did he say ports in New Mexico? Could this be a wharf story?

Well, not exactly, these are Ports of Entry from Mexico and Texas. Trucks, not ships. Yet several issues seem to mirroe Port Police ChiefRobert Pierce's challenges in Galveston.

I'm in Roswell, New Mexico, where I traveled with our son Charles in his Ford pickup, not a space ship. With his travel and work schedule if we wanted to visit it meant a trip to Roswell. As a young boy, he used to travel with me to Santa Fe, the capital, where he listened while I met with the governor and legislature.

Now, as Deputy Director of the Legislative Finance Committee (LFC), he evaluates state agency programs, writing reports to inform the policy makers. As the Chair of the Committee, Senator John Arthur Smith said, "With a part-time volunteer citizen legislature, the LFC plays a critical role for the state, including drafting the budget each year. We could not do our jobs without them."

The legislators always generously compliment me on Charles. As a result, we have switched roles. He used to be introduced as "Alvin's son," now it's, "This is Charles's dad."

After the hearing, we made field trips in a very dry 104 degrees (still felt cooler than 80 degrees in Galveston) to Eastern New Mexico University-Roswell, and to huge hangars where airline planes are painted and repaired.

Alongside the hangars is the longest three-foot thick runway in the United States—2.5 miles. Actually, the President landed here this afternoon in Air Force One to visit Carlsbad Caverns, celebrating the 100th anniversary of the National Parks. Other venues are world-class art museums. This is Wyeth and Hurd country.

One could see Roswell and Galveston as complete opposites but I see similar themes. Both towns have been hit by disasters. Galveston's are natural; Roswell's was the closing of the huge Walker Air Force Base in 1967, an economic disaster. Today, led by active Mayor Dennis Kintigh and the University administration, Roswell has grown to 67,000 folks, with well-paying jobs and a low cost of living. Like Galveston, tourism is up—New Mexico True.

While the ports may differ, Galveston and Roswell both have public and private folks working hard to create economic development and jobs. During dinner, I sat between the ranking Democratic and Republican Senators. It was clear they were interested in governing and addressing the State's problems, a striking difference from my spring visit to D.C. Something to keep in mind during the next election season.

Nice place to visit, friendly folks with lots of sandy beaches, but no ocean and the docks are much smaller.

Take me back to Galveston.

Other Readings

For more about Galveston and its connection to the sea, I recommend:

Galveston: A History by David G. McComb,
University of Texas-Austin Press, 1986.

Bill Cherry's Galveston Memories, by William Cherry.
VanJus Press, Galveston, Texas, 2000.

Galveston's Red Light District: A History of the Line,
by Kimber Fountain, History Press, Charleston, So. Carolina, 2018.

Galveston and the Civil War: An Island City in the Maelstrom by James M. Schmidt. History Press, Charleston, So. Carolina, 2012.

Handbook of Texas Online, by Edward Coyle Sealy, *Galveston Wharves* www.tshaonline.org/handbook/online/articles/etg01

Ray Miller's Galveston, by Ray Miller. Capital Printing,
Austin, Texas 1983.

Recalled Recollections by I. H. Kempner. The Egan Company,
Dallas Texas, 1981.

Women, Culture and Community by Elizabeth Hayes Turner
Oxford Press, New York, 1997.

Galveston: A History of the Island by Gary Cartwright.
Atheneum, New York, 1991.

The Storm of the Century by Al Roker.
Harper Collins, New York, 2015.

Texas Almanac 2014-2015, Editor Elizabeth Cruce Alvarez.
Texas State Historical Association. Texas A&M Press,
College Station, Texas, 2014.

Caribbean, by James A. Michener. Random House, NY, 1989.

Made in the USA
Monee, IL
04 March 2024

54186188R00125